The nude and pierced bodies of the Grimes
Sisters were found today in a scraggy stretch
of freshly thawed land along a highway
southwest of Chicago. Police said the girls
appeared to have been dead about two weeks.
**Associated Press: January 22, 1957**

If you're good Presley fans, you'll go home and ease your mother's worries.
**Elvis Presley, in a statement from Graceland**

The murderer in this case is diabolically clever. He used a method which we are unable to detect. Perhaps he is a person trained in chemistry with a knowledge of unusual poisons.
**Dr. Jerry K. Kearns**

There were marks of violence on the girls' faces. I know that, and the police know that, too.
**Harry Glos**

It's a lie! It's a lie! My daughters wouldn't go to West Madison Street. They didn't know where it was. My daughters were good girls.
**Loretta Grimes**

Six years ago today, I killed Barbara and Patricia Grimes and I've been running ever since.
**Alfred Smith Lawless, 1962**

Dead Men Do Tell Tales Series

# THE TWO LOST GIRLS

## THE MYSTERY OF THE GRIMES SISTERS

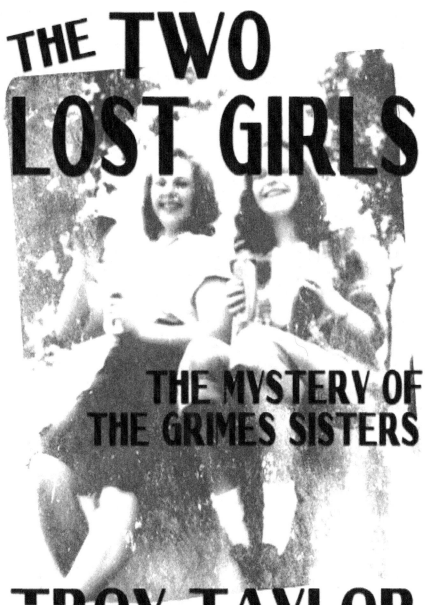

# TROY TAYLOR

**Original Cover Artwork Designed by**
© Copyright 2015 by April Slaughter & Troy Taylor

**This Book is Published By:**
Whitechapel Press
American Hauntings Ink
Jacksonville, Illinois | 217.791.7859
Visit us on the Internet at http://www.whitechapelpress.com

First Edition - November 2015
ISBN: 1-892523-98-1


Printed in the United States of America

# ALONG A SNOW-COVERED ROAD

With the way that the sun rose so brightly over the Chicago landscape on January 22, 1957, no one could have predicted the dark day that was ahead. It was a cold, clear morning and the bright sun reflected off the snow-covered hills and trees of the city's far southwest side. The tall buildings of Chicago's downtown seemed far off in the distance for small towns like Willow Springs, which had sprung up along the Des Plaines River and the old Illinois & Michigan Canal in the 1830s. It had remained an isolated country town for more than a century and didn't even have its own police department until 1952. Five years later, the small community would gain national attention for the gruesome discovery made on that January day.

Around 1:00 p.m. on that Tuesday afternoon, Leonard Prescott, a 39 year-old construction worker from Hinsdale, was driving east on German Church Road, a country roadway just outside of Willow Springs. He was on his way into town to do some shopping and was probably thinking of little other than the grocery list that his wife had given him before he left the house. He was driving slowly along the wooded, rural road, mindful of the snow-packed pavement and the ice that was lurking beneath. There had been several snows already in the New Year; the last only a few days before. He drove down a small hill and then crossed a bridge over Devil's Creek, a small tributary that was about 200 yards east of the DuPage County Line Road. From his car, Prescott could see under and beyond the bridge railing. There was a flat piece of snow-covered ground there that extended for only about 10 feet before dropping off steeply to the creek below.

Prescott later said, "I didn't have a care in the world. My wife told me to go out and get groceries. I was going mighty slow and I noticed these flesh-colored things underneath the railing."

Reflexively, Prescott tapped the brake of his car and the tires crunched to a stop on the snow. He leaned over and tried to get a better look at the strange objects. He never got out of the car. Looking closer, he told himself that the shapes were department store mannequins, which someone had tossed out on the side of the road.

He put the car back into gear and drove off, intent on going to the grocery store. He never made it.

Prescott was unable to get the image of the shapes on the side of the road out of his head. There was no use in trying to shop for groceries. He had a terrible feeling about what he had caught a glimpse of in the snow. He and his wife Marie had seen the newspapers stories about the two missing girls. What if...?

He sped back home and hurried into the house. Marie Prescott later said that he was greatly agitated and upset.

"My god, I can't believe what I just saw! You've got to come with me and look!" he told her.

Marie, who worked as a machine operator at night and cared for the Prescotts' five children by day - including a preschooler crippled by polio - was not excited about the idea of leaving the house to go and look at something. She had children who would soon be home from school and still needed to get ready to go to work that night.

But something in her husband's eyes convinced her to go with him. Together, they drove back to the bridge on German Church Road and this time, Prescott got out of the car. Marie followed him and then froze about fifteen feet away from the two shapes in the snow. There was no question about what Leonard had seen - the "mannequins" were actually the pale, naked bodies of two young women. Tinged with blue against the white backdrop of the snow, one of the girls lay on her left side with her legs slightly drawn up toward her body. Her head was covered by the other girl, who had been thrown onto her back with her head turned sharply to the right. It looked as if they had been discarded there by someone so cold and heartless that he saw the girls as nothing more than refuse to be tossed away on a lonely roadside.

Marie Prescott let out a choked scream and collapsed on the roadway. She could not believe what she was seeing. Weeping inconsolably, Leonard had to carry her back to the car. Once she was settled into the passenger's seat, the stunned couple quickly drove to the Willow Springs police station, which was less than a mile away. As they pulled in, they encountered Sergeant John Alexander McKay, a two-year veteran, who was arriving at the same time.

Sergeant McKay later testified: "I was just going to get out of the car, when this man, Leonard Prescott, came alongside. He was all excited, said he'd seen two dummies lying alongside the road on German Church Road along County Line Road. I told him that I would immediately go over there, he should show me the spot. When I got near there, he stayed about fifteen feet from the line of the incline. I went down and I noticed the bodies behind the guardrail alongside of a ravine. I climbed out and looked over the ravine and I seen that there were two nude girls, I guess about thirteen or fifteen years of age, somewhere around there."

McKay immediately got into his car and radioed the information to the sheriff's police. Like Prescott, he was shaken by what he had seen and he also had a terrible feeling that the two dead girls were connected to the reports of the two young women who had gone missing back in December. After he made his call to the sheriff's department, he stood watch over the scene and waited for the official authorities to take over.

Just who was actually in charge of the case would soon come into question, but police officers from various departments - county, city, and nearby suburbs - rapidly descended on the scene. The father of the two missing girls, a man named Joseph Grimes, was led to the site to make a positive identification. Bracing himself for what he was about to see, officers led him to the ground on the other side of the guardrail. He looked down at the two bodies and choked out a few words, "Yes, they are my daughters," before he burst into tears and slumped limply to the ground.

Barbara and Patricia Grimes, missing since December 28, had been found. Their puzzling disappearance had become two unexplainable deaths. Since that time, it has become one of Chicago's most heartbreaking unsolved crimes and the event that shattered the innocence of Chicago forever.

# THE TWO LOST GIRLS

On December 28, 1956, and Patricia Grimes, 13, and Barbara Grimes, 15, left their home at 3624 South Damen Avenue and headed for the Brighton Theater, only a mile away on Archer Avenue. The girls were both avid fans of Elvis Presley and on that night were on their way to see his film *Love Me Tender* for the eleventh, and what would be their final, time. The girls were recognized in the popcorn line at 9:30 p.m. and then seen on an eastbound Archer Avenue bus at 11:00 p.m. After that, things are less certain, but this may have been the last time they were ever seen alive. The two sisters were missing for twenty-five days, before their naked and frozen bodies were found along German Church Road, just outside the small town of Willow Springs.

Things like that just didn't happen on Chicago's Southwest Side in 1957.

The Grimes sisters grew up in the McKinley Park neighborhood, west of Bridgeport and east of Brighton Park. It took its name from the huge park that made up the area's southern boundary. Once known as the Brighton Park Race Track, by the middle 1950s, it boasted the city's largest tennis club and a swimming pool. The local kids loved the park in the summertime, taking part in craft classes, playing baseball or getting burgers and Cokes from Lindy's, which was at the intersection of Western and Archer Avenues. At this same intersection was a statue of the man for whom the park was named, fallen president William McKinley.

McKinley Park was a blue collar, working-class neighborhood, where dreams of steady jobs and regular paychecks were still coming true in the 1950s. More than seventy years before, there were nearly thirty brick-making yards on the banks of the Chicago River, and around 1900, William Wrigley built a chewing gum factory at 35th Street and Ashland Avenue, right in the middle of America's first planned industrial park. The park, a joint venture of the Chicago Union Stockyards and the Chicago Junction Railway, was followed by a post-World War I peak in the meatpacking industry. These

8

industries, along with the *Chicago Sun-Times* publishing and distribution plant west of Ashland along the river, meant there was no shortage of jobs for the Bohemian, Polish, Irish, and German communities in the area.

A large number of these immigrants, and children of immigrants, settled McKinley Park in the early 1900s. By the 1950s, the local industries were still thriving. In spite of the many changes that came after World War II, Chicago was still a factory town. Paychecks, which averaged about $90 a week in McKinley Park, went to pay for tickets to the Riverview Amusement Park at Belmont and Western Avenues, or bought school clothes from Sears at 63rd and Halsted Streets, or from Goldblatts at 47th and Ashland. At Archer and Kedzie was the Archer Big Store, where just about anything could be found.

Archer Avenue, which slices through the southwest side and continues on an angle all of the way out to Lemont, was an old Indian trail that became a road when it was used to build the Illinois & Michigan Canal. Not only did it carry McKinley Park residents to the forest preserves outside of the city for recreation, it also offered a quick commute to Chicago's downtown, where many residents found additional employment opportunities. Businesses in the Loop required clerical workers, mostly female, to keep their offices running and uniformed operators, mostly male, to park the cars and run the elevators, which had not yet been automated.

Shopping in downtown Chicago held great appeal in the 1950s, especially since the stores stayed open as late as 8:30 p.m. on weeknights. Modest budgets still allowed for sales at Marshall Field or dinners at one of Tad's steakhouses, where cooks grilled a New York strip, accompanied by a salad and a baked potato, for just $1.29. The easy access that McKinley Park offered to the city allowed residents to spend the evening out and still be home at a reasonable hour.

Sunday was still a day of rest and reverence in the 1950s. McKinley Park Lutherans attended St. Andrew, which had its own small bowling alley that was open to the public, and the German St. Philippus. Catholics, which far outnumbered the other residents, were divided among three parishes - St. Peter and Paul, Our Lady of Good Counsel, and St. Maurice, where the Grimes family worshipped and where Barbara and Patricia had attended the parish school.

9

McKinley Park was a decent place for a kid to grow up in the 1950s. It was not a place where young girls were kidnapped and murdered - at least it wasn't before the last days of 1956.

Friday, December 28, was a typical winter day in Chicago. There was dirty snow on the ground, a chill in the air, and the weather forecasts called for bad weather in the days to come. For Barbara and Patricia Grimes, though, it was a special day. Elvis Presley's movie *Love Me Tender* had completed its downtown run and had arrived at their neighborhood theater, the Brighton, at 4223 South Archer Avenue. The theater was a short ride away for the girls on the #62 bus, which they caught on Archer Avenue, just two blocks from their home on South Damen. Like many young girls of the era, Barbara and Patricia were enthralled with Elvis. They had recently joined his fan club and were just waiting for their membership confirmations to arrive in the mail. By the time that *Love Me Tender* began its run at the Brighton Theater on December 28, the sisters had already seen the movie 10 times. On this night, they would see it for the last time.

Barbara Jeanne Grimes had been born on May 5, 1941. Her sister, Patricia Kathleen, was born less than two years later on December 31, 1943. Their parents, Joseph and Loretta Grimes, had been married in July 1924 when Joseph was barely seventeen years old and ten months younger than his bride. Their first child, Shirley, was born in 1926, followed by Leona in 1928. They would eventually have seven children altogether. Joseph and Loretta separated when their youngest child was still an infant, leaving the day-to-day responsibilities of parenting to Loretta.

Their divorce was an uncomplicated one, filed in December 1951. In the terms of the agreement, Joseph was ordered to pay $150 in attorney's fees and $35 per week in child support for the two girls and their three siblings who still lived at home. This was a substantial part of his $80 a week paycheck as a truck driver for Bozzy Cartage on South Washtenaw Avenue. At the time his daughters disappeared, Joseph was living in a large yellow brick apartment building at 2739 West 61st Street with his second wife, Grace, whom he had married in August of 1956.

Loretta Grimes worked long hours as a file clerk at Parke-Davis Pharmaceuticals, but the family was reportedly on welfare for at least part of Barbara and Patricia's early lives - often going without

*Barbara (Left) and Patricia (Right) Grimes*

heat and lights. There was no question that she was a devoted mother, though. When not working, she was always with her children. She once stated that what the family lacked in money, they made up for in love.

Even though she was younger than her sister, Patricia Grimes was the spunkier and more outgoing of the two. She was three inches taller than her older sister and was looking forward to not only the Elvis movie on Friday night, but a small party with several girlfriends on Saturday night to celebrate her birthday, which was actually two days later. She was in the seventh grade at the St. Maurice parish school, located at 36th Street and Hoyne Avenue, right around the corner from the Grimes house.

Barbara, the quieter of the two girls, had attended all eight years of grade school at St. Maurice and was a sophomore at Kelly High School in 1956. To help out with household expenses, she worked part-time at Wolf Furniture House on Archer Avenue. Barbara and Patricia, seemingly inseparable, often walked places hand in hand.

Before going to the movies on Friday evening, the two girls had a dinner of tuna fish and potatoes, common fare for Catholics on Friday in those days. It was Barbara who talked their mother into allowing the two of them to see the movie. Even though she had been taking medicine for a bad cough, she begged Loretta for permission. Mrs. Grimes reluctantly agreed and gave Barbara $2.50, instructing her to put 50 cents in the zipper of her wallet to save for the bus ride home. The sisters ate chocolate chip cookies for dessert and at 7:15 kissed their mother goodbye as they prepared to leave for the theater.

It was the last time that Loretta would ever see the girls alive.

Loretta expected the girls to be home by 11:45 p.m., which would have allowed them to watch the movie twice, but was already growing uneasy when they had not arrived 15 minutes prior to that. At midnight, she sent her daughter Theresa, 17, and her son, Joey, 14, to the bus stop at 35th and Hoyne to watch for them. After three buses had stopped and had failed to discharge their sisters, Theresa and Joey returned home without them. At that point, Loretta called the police.

At 12:30 a.m., Officer Herman Steinberg of the Brighton Park station met Theresa and Joey at Archer and Damen Avenues. Joey explained to Officer Steinberg that his sisters were missing, which got more attention in those days than a similar report would get today. Steinberg took a description of the girls and alerted all of the officers in the district on midnight patrol. About 2:00 a.m., Mrs. Grimes called the squad room and reported the disappearance again. Her daughters had attended a movie, she told the officer who answered the telephone, and they had never come home. He took the description of the girls and sent it out on the wire again.

The following morning, juvenile officers, policewomen, and District 20 detectives started an investigation. By Monday, which was New Year's Eve and Patricia's birthday, Chicago newspapers were carrying the story of the girls' disappearance, and the police were setting up a special task force to look for them. They canvassed door-to-door throughout the neighborhood and searched alleys, garages, outbuildings, and basements. Officers checked what seemed to be every inch of the area bounded by 51st Street, the drainage canal, Chicago River and Laramie Avenue. Railroad detectives joined the search of the Santa Fe Railroad yards, worried that the girls might have locked themselves in one of the freight cars. The police sent circulars to all of the precincts in the city, as well as to law enforcement agencies across the country.

*Schoolchildren at St. Maurice folded and mailed "missing" flyers with photos and descriptions of the Grimes sisters.*

The girls' Elvis Presley fan club membership cards arrived at the family home as the search continued. As their disappearances became national news, even Elvis himself issued a statement from Graceland. "If you're good Presley fans," he tried to appeal to them, "you'll go home and ease your mother's worries." But if the girls had run away from home, even Elvis was unable to get them to return.

Meanwhile, as Joseph Grimes was enlisting fellow truck drivers to search for the girls on the road, students at St. Maurice volunteered to send out more than 15,000 flyers to area homes. The clergy and the parishioners from the church offered a $1,000 reward for information, hoping that someone might have seen the girls before they vanished. Even photographs were taken of friends of the girls that duplicated the clothing they wore on December 28, in hopes that it might jog the memory of someone who saw them. On the night they went to the movies for the last time, Patricia wore blue jeans, a yellow sweater, a black jacket with white sleeve stripes, a white scarf over her head and black shoes. Her sister reportedly wore a gray tweed skirt, yellow blouse, a three-quarter-length coat, a gray

scarf, white bobby sox and black ballerina shoes. None of the girls' clothing was ever found, although some time after it was learned that they were dead, a yellow sweater, thought to be Patricia's was found in a stone building in a park about a half mile from where their bodies turned up. It was examined by Loretta Grimes, but she said that it was not Patricia's.

The residents of the Chicago area were stunned and the two lost girls became an obsession. The local community organized a search for clues and volunteers passed out flyers looking for information. Money was raised to assist the Grimes family and eventually the funds paid off Loretta's Damen Avenue home.

*Photos were taken of the Grimes sister's friends, dressed in the same outfits they had been wearing when they disappeared with the hope that it might jog the memory of a witness.*

But all of this activity and obsession was designed to hide one thing - bone-chilling fear. At a time when most parents were still worried about their children coming down with polio, no one was prepared for the disappearance of two innocent girls - any more than they had been prepared for the brutal murders of three young boys just a little over a year before. The disappearance of the Grimes sisters was the second in what became a string of dead children in Chicago in the 1950s. They became stories that not only shaped the childhoods of a generation, but officially marked the end of innocence in Chicago.

# THE THREE LOST BOYS

In October 1955, more than a year before the Grimes sisters vanished from the city's southwest side, the bodies of the three boys were discovered in a virtually crime-free community on the northwest side of Chicago. The Schuessler-Peterson murders, as they came to be called, shocked the entire city and were the first murders of the 1950s that changed Chicago forever.

The terrifying events began on a cool Sunday afternoon in the fall of 1955 when three boys from the northwest side of the city headed downtown to catch a matinee performance of a Walt Disney nature film called *The African Lion* at the Loop Theater. The boys made the trip with their parents' consent because in those days, parents thought little of their responsible children going off on excursions by themselves. The boys had always proven dependable in the past and this time would have been no exception, if tragedy had not occurred. Bobby Peterson's mother had chosen the film for he and his two friends, Anton and John Schuessler, and had sent them on their way with $4 in loose change between them. It should have been plenty of money to keep them occupied for an afternoon and safely get them back home again.

What happened when the movie ended, though, is a still a time shrouded in mystery.

The matinee ended that afternoon but for some reason, at around 6:00 p.m. that evening, the boys were reported seen in the lobby of the Garland Building at 111 North Wabash. There was no explanation for what they might have been doing there, other than that Bobby's eye doctor had an office in the building. It seems unlikely that he would have been visiting the optometrist on a Sunday afternoon, but his signature did appear on the lobby registry for that day, so he was obviously there. The Garland did have a reputation in those days for being a hangout for gays, prostitutes and hustlers, but if that had anything to do with the boys being there, no one knows.

Some have surmised that they only stopped long enough to use the restroom since Bobby knew there was one available on the ninth floor, where his optometrist's office was located. They may have

*Bobby Peterson (Left) and the Schuessler Brothers, Anton and John. They vanished in October 1955.*

hurried up to the ninth floor and then went right back out again because they were only believed to be at the Garland for less than five minutes.

Around 7:45 p.m., the three entered the Monte Cristo Bowling Alley at 3226 West Montrose Avenue. The parlor was a neighborhood eating place and the proprietor later recalled to the police that he remembered seeing the boys and that a "fifty-ish" looking man was showing an "abnormal interest" in several younger boys who were bowling. He was unable to say if this man had contact with the trio. They left the bowling alley and walked down Montrose to another bowling alley, but were turned away here because a league had taken over all of the available lanes for the evening.

Out of money, but for some reason not headed toward home, the boys hitched a ride at the intersection of Lawrence and Milwaukee Avenue. It was now 9:05 p.m. and their parents were beginning to get worried. They had reason to be -- for the boys were never seen alive again.

Two days later, the boys' naked and bound bodies were discovered in a shallow ditch, near a parking lot about 100 feet east

*The Robinson Woods Indian Burial Grounds, where the boys'
bodies were discovered.*

of the Des Plaines River. A salesman, who had stopped to eat his
lunch at the Robinson Wood's Indian Burial Grounds nearby, spotted
them and called the police. Coroner Walter McCarron stated that
the cause of death was "asphyxiation by suffocation." The three boys
had been dead about thirty-six hours when they were discovered. He
also declared that the killing had been a "sex crime" and the work
of a "madman" or a "teen gang." It was, he stated, "the most horrible
sex crime in years."

Bobby Peterson had been struck repeatedly and had been
strangled with a rope or a necktie. Newspaper reports said that he
had been slashed across the head 14 times with a knife or an ax.
The Schuessler brothers, it appeared, had been strangled by hand
and had been hit on their faces with what appeared to be the flat
side of a knife. The killer had used adhesive tape to cover the eyes
of all three victims. They had then been dragged or thrown from a
vehicle. Their clothing was never discovered.

The city of Chicago was thrown into a panic. Police officials reported that they had never seen such a horrible crime. The fears of parents all over the city were summed up by the shaken Anton Schuessler, Sr. who said, "When you get to the point that children cannot go to the movies in the afternoon and get home safely, something is wrong with this country."

Police officers combed the area, conducting door-to-door searches and neighborhood interrogations. Search teams combed Robinson's Woods, looking for clues or items of clothing. The killer (or killers) had gone to great lengths to get rid of any fingerprints or traces of evidence. More than one hundred officers, joined by fifty soldiers from the nearby Army anti-aircraft base, gathered near Robinson Woods at daybreak and walked in lines spaced four or

*The frenzied crime scene at Robinson's Woods. Within hours of the bodies being discovered, any possible clues were destroyed by well-intentioned police officers and volunteers.*

# HUNT STRANGLER OF 3 BOYS

## *Naked Bodies Found in Ditch in Woods*

**MISSING PUPILS DEAD 36 HOURS; EYES AND MOUTHS OF ALL TAPED**

ROBERT PETERSON    JOHN SCHUESSLER    ANTON SCHUESSLER JR.

One of Victims Beaten with Tire Iron or Butt of Gun; Find Fingernail Marks on Throats of Two

*The public was stunned by the crime. October 19, 1955 newspaper stories stated: "The naked, mutilated bodies of three boys were found piled in a forest ditch yesterday. Authorities called their slaying one of the Chicago area's most brutal in history and blamed it on either a madman or a gang of older youths."*

five feet apart, looking for anything out of place. Divers were sent into the depths of the Des Plaines River for clues, but found nothing.

By this time, various city and suburban police departments had descended on the scene, running into each other and further hampering the search for clues. There was little or no cooperation between the separate agencies, and if anything had been discovered, it would have most likely been lost in the confusion.

Away from the scene, patrolmen and detectives conducted a huge roundup of known "sex deviates," especially those known to work in, or frequent, bowling alleys. They were convinced that this was where the boys had come into contact with the killer or killers. Most of the cops were convinced that a "gang" of some sort had been at work, finding it hard to believe that all three boys could have been killed otherwise. Coroner McCarron extended the possibility that they "fell into the hands of a group of older boys and were manhandled."

While the city remained in stunned shock, the investigation stumbled along under the leadership of Cook County Sheriff Joseph D. Lohman, who searched in desperation for some answers in the case. He even offered $2,500 from his personal bank account for information leading to an arrest. Lohman was over his head with the baffling case and he found himself under unwanted scrutiny by the newspapers, which sensationalized the murders, and the general public, which was collectively terrified.

Lohman was quoted in the press as stating: "Chances are that the attackers were persons close to the boys' own age, who might have known them." He also pointed to indications that the victims had been held captive before they were killed and may have been slain because something had "gone wrong" and the captors wanted to make sure they were not identified. He said that Bobby, who took the worst beating, might have been killed first.

Not to leave out any possible theories, though, Lohman also took things in another direction and later, he also surmised that the slayer was a "burly madman" or that two men had committed the crime. He noted that the "bodies had been thrown like bags of potatoes" and that this "would suggest that at least two persons or one very powerful person did it."

The first suspect picked up in the case was an unemployed schoolteacher, who was brought in for questioning early in the morning. He lived five blocks from the Schuessler home and had been named in an anonymous telephone call to the police. He was questioned vigorously, but after offering to take a lie detector test, was released. He would not be the last "person of interest" to be questioned in the case, but time after time, the men were interrogated and let go.

While investigators were coming up empty, newspaper reporters hounded the grief-stricken parents of the three boys. The press descended on their neighborhood of modest bungalow homes, a place where crime of any kind was rare. It was almost impossible for them to even fathom what had occurred. Murder was something that happened in the newspapers, not in their own homes.

Mrs. Schuessler, described as a "frail 37 year-old woman," rocked back and forth on her living room couch on the day the bodies were found, surrounded by friends and neighbors. Reporters pushed into the room, looking for comments, but she only murmured things

*The grieving Anton Schuessler, Sr. was just forty-one years old at the time of the murders. He died of a heart attack one month later. His widow, Eleanor, remarried but died in 1986, still hoping for closure.*

like, "My life, my arms... my legs... now gone." Once she shrieked out, "I want my boys! I want my...." before collapsing into hysterics.

Mr. Schuessler rushed into the room and fell to his knees in front of the couch where his wife was sitting. He shuddered with pain and apparent agony. "Mother, mother," he cried. "What kind of land do we live in?" He buried his face in her lap and sobbed.

The investigation continued with no results while the last days of Bobby Peterson and Anton and John Schuessler ended on a grim note. An honor guard of Boy Scouts carried the coffins of the three boys from the St. Tarcissus Roman Catholic Church to a hearse that would take them to St. Joseph Cemetery. The church was filled to capacity with an estimated 1,200 mourners and even more people joined the families at the graveside service, numbering over 3,500. Reverend Raymond G. Carey told the gathering, "God has permitted sin, evil and suffering because He knows that He can bring good from the suffering." But no one present could see much in the way of good from the deaths of three innocent young boys.

The Schuessler-Peterson murders were barely out of the headlines when the Grimes sisters disappeared. Dorothy Peterson, Bobby's mother, sent a sympathy card to Loretta Grimes after the girls' bodies were found. "It isn't safe for children to be on the streets anymore," she wrote.

A lot of fathers and mothers shared this sense of foreboding. The age of innocence was over, they believed; America was changing for the worse.

Unlike the unsolved murders of the Grimes sisters, however, the killer of Bobby Peterson and the Schuessler brothers was surprisingly brought to justice four decades after the murders were committed.

Many years passed. As there is no statute of limitations for murder, the Schuessler-Peterson case officially remained open, but there seemed to be little chance that it would ever be solved. The murders became sort of a cautionary tale in the Chicago area, painting a bloody picture of what happened when children talked to strangers.

Then, forty years later, and long after the principals in the case had passed away, a bizarre turn of events occurred that would finally offer closure for the cold case. In the middle 1990s, a government informant named William "Red" Wemette accused a man named Kenneth Hansen of the murders during a police investigation into the 1977 disappearance of candy heiress Helen Vorhees Brach.

In 1955, Hansen, then twenty-two years old, worked as a stable hand for Silas Jayne, a millionaire from Kane County. Jayne himself was wild and reckless and had been suspected of many violent and devious dealings during his rise to power in the horse-breeding world. He went to prison in 1973 for the murder of his half-brother, George, and died of leukemia in 1987, escaping punishment for many of the crimes that were later laid at his doorstep.

Hansen had certainly committed plenty of crimes himself. The homosexual hustler would later admit to molesting scores of young boys and investigators were easily able to build a case against him, thanks to missing pieces filled in by Wemette and other informants.

In the summer of 1994, sensing the investigation was closing in on him, Hansen attempted to leave town, only to be arrested on an

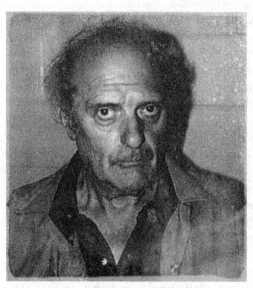

**Kenneth Hansen in 1995**

arson charge in a 1972 fire at a suburban Chicago stable. He was charged later the same day with killing the boys.

The police believed that Hansen picked the boys up as they hitchhiked on Milwaukee Avenue south of Lawrence Avenue. He lived nearby at the time, in the 5000 block of North Claremont Avenue. Hansen then drove the boys to Idle Hour Stables, 8600 Higgins Rd. on the city's Northwest Side, where he either worked or frequently visited. His story was that he wanted to show the boys some prize horses that were being kept at the stables. Once there, he tried to pay the boys to perform a sex act, sources said. When they refused, he became violent, raped, and then murdered the boys, according to the sources to which Hansen later bragged. After killing them, he loaded up the bodies and dumped them at Robinson Woods with help from his brother.

In the spring of 1956, the Idle Hours Stables burned to the ground. The week before the fire, the Cook County Coroner announced to the press that he planned to exhume the bodies of the three boys in a search for trace evidence. Silas Jayne, after seeing the newspaper report, became convinced that remnants of his stables might remain on the boys. Police detectives had previously visited the stable as they followed up on reports of boy's screams coming from the building at night. Jayne thought they might put it all together and Hansen's crime would bring him down. Out of fear, he torched the building to obliterate all of the evidence. This was standard operating procedure for Jayne, as he would later be accused of burning stables and killing horses to collect insurance payments. In this case, detectives at the time never connected the fire to the murders and Hansen escaped arrest and prosecution for nearly forty years.

After the arrest, authorities refused to reveal what hard evidence they had against Hansen. Sources said, however, that most of the evidence came from people who somehow learned of the crime over the years. "After 40 years go by, you don't solve a case by physical evidence," Cook County State's Attorney Jack O'Malley said at a press conference announcing the charges.

As the case came to trial in 1995, four decades of silence were broken as many of Hansen's other victims came forward, recalling promises of jobs made to young men in return for sexual favors. He forced their silence with threats that included warnings that they might end up "like the Peterson boy."

Though the evidence against him mostly consisted of testimony from people who claimed he'd told them about killing the boys, and there was no physical evidence or eyewitness testimony to corroborate the prosecution's allegations against him, a Cook County jury convicted Kenneth Hansen of the murders in September 1995. They deliberated for less than two hours and Hansen was sentenced to two hundred years in prison.

But the case was not yet over. In May 2000, the Illinois Appellate Court overturned Hansen's conviction. Two of the three justices found that the judge in the case erred when he allowed evidence to be submitted that showed that Hansen regularly picked up hitchhikers and sexually abused them. In spite of his original verdict being overturned, Hansen was almost routinely convicted again, and once more, he received the two-hundred-year sentence. The verdict was affirmed on appeal in 2004. Hansen died behind bars in September 2007, and after what became nearly fifty years, Bobby, John and Anton could finally rest in peace.

But the same could not be said for Barbara and Patricia Grimes.

# MISSING

Frantic days passed. As people across the Chicago area were doing everything that they could to try and find the two missing sisters, Barbara and Patricia were, it seemed, being spotted everywhere - and nowhere.

The last confirmed sighting of the two girls came from a classmate who sat with them at the first showing of *Love Me Tender* at the Brighton Theater. Dorothy Weinert left after the first viewing of the film because her six year-old sister, Jeanette, had fallen asleep. They left on the bus and were home ten minutes later. Dorothy had no idea anything was wrong until the following morning, when Joey Grimes banged on the family's front door and asked if they had seen his sisters.

The police had no reason to doubt Dorothy's sighting, since the girls had planned to go to the movies, but subsequent sightings, which poured in on a daily basis while the police searched for the sisters, were not so definite. Many of them were very strange, seemingly impossible, covering almost the entire Chicago area.

*The Brighton Theater on Archer Avenue. The Grimes sisters attended the theater that night and then vanished while on their way home.*

A Chicago Transit Authority bus driver named Joseph Smok thought they left his bus at Archer and Western Avenues at 11:05 p.m. on the night they vanished. While this would have been the correct route for the girls, this intersection was several blocks away from their home and would have meant that they exited the bus a few stops early. Smok believed that he heard the two girls say they were hoping to catch the oncoming northbound Western Avenue trolley, which was the wrong direction if they had been heading home.

The next sighting allegedly occurred on December 29, the morning after they disappeared. Jack Franklin, a security guard on the northwest side of Chicago, offered directions to two girls that he later identified as Barbara and Patricia. He passed by them near Lawrence and Central Park Avenues, a little more than twelve hours after they left the theater. He only remembered them, he said, because they were so rude - something that friends of the girls disputed. They were wondering aloud where to catch the bus, and when he pointed to a nearby stop, one of them told him to "shut up." Oddly, this sighting supposedly took place almost exactly where the Schuessler-Peterson boys were last seen alive in October 1955.

Also on December 29, Judy Burrow, 15, a friend of Barbara Grimes, reported to Captain John McCarthy of the Brighton Park police station that she had seen the sisters at 2:30 p.m. that afternoon, walking west on Archer Avenue, two blocks west of Damen Avenue.

More than twenty-four hours after their disappearance, Patricia's classmate, Catherine Borak, was eating at Angelo's Restaurant at 3551 South Archer Avenue and thought she saw Patricia walk past the window with two girls that she didn't recognize. This sighting was followed by another, six hours later, by a cashier at the Clark Theater in downtown Chicago, who claimed she saw both girls at 12:45 a.m.

Later that same afternoon, a railroad conductor named Bernard Norton thought the two girls were on his train near the Great Lakes Naval Training Center in north suburban Glenview. This seemed like a worthwhile tip because the police had been searching for two sailors, "Terry" and "Larry." The girls had reportedly met the two young men downtown at the Oriental Theater in November, where Love Me Tender had been showing. At some point, Barbara and Patricia had brought the boys home with them and Loretta Grimes

27

had served them coffee and cake. She recalled that the last telephone contact that the girls had with the young men was on November 28. The train sighting led nowhere.

On January 1, the two missing girls were allegedly seen again on a city bus. Driver Robert Curran from Cicero identified them as passengers on his Damen Avenue route.

During the next week, several people in Englewood reported seeing the Grimes sisters. George Pope, a night clerk at the Unity Hotel on West 61st Place, said that two girls fitting the sisters' description requested a room on either December 29 or December 30 - he couldn't remember which night it had been - at around 9:00 p.m. All of the rooms at the hotel were full at the time, but Pope claimed he would have refused them anyway because they were too young.

On January 3, the connection between the sisters and two sailors came up again when three employees at the Kresge "five and dime" store at 63rd and Halsted insisted that they saw the girls playing Elvis records on the store player with two men in Navy uniforms. Chicago police Lieutenant Donald Keevers said that this report was one of the "most convincing" he heard. His son, Tom, later recalled a number of people who came to the Keevers' house with other sightings that weren't nearly as legitimate. "Once a woman came to our door and said that she'd seen the girls in the bark of a tree," he said. "But my dad was always polite."

On one cold night in early January, an unknown telephone caller told Theresa Grimes that her sisters' bodies had been dumped in the garbage cans behind the Brighton Theater. Panicked, she called the police, but officers searched the alley behind the building and didn't turn up anything.

The cruel telephone calls would continue throughout the search and even long after it was discovered that the girls were dead. One night, a young girl telephoned the Grimes home and when Loretta answered, the voice on the other end of the line cried, "It's Petey! This is Petey!" Then the caller hung up. "Petey" was Patricia's family nickname. Reporters later stated that Loretta "cried for an hour" after the prank call.

On January 5, a junk dealer in Iroquois County, Illinois called the Chicago police and reported seeing the girls in the town of Gilman, about ninety miles south of the city. He said they were in a maroon,

28

1947 automobile with Tennessee plates and a Chicago vehicle sticker. Nothing came from this sighting either.

At this point, Captain John McCarthy said he believed that the girls were still in the area, close to home. Even though Loretta Grimes adamantly believed otherwise, he still thought they had run away. Mrs. Grimes did not agree. "I don't think my girls have run away," she said. "If there was any way for them to get home, I know they would. They are not the type of girls to run away."

She told reporters that on the night of December 28, Barbara had given her mother a paycheck of $20.25 and her Christmas bonus of $5 from Wolf Furniture to help with the family's household expenses. "Does that sound like a girl who is going to run away?" she asked. She also showed them identical gifts that her daughters had received for Christmas - portable radios in leather cases. "If they had wanted to go away, they would have taken these," she said with strong assurance.

A letter to advice columnist Ann Landers seemed to agree with what Mrs. Grimes was telling reporters and the police. The letter was reportedly written by a young girl who had been at the movie on the same night as Barbara and Patricia. It read:

*Betty asked me to go with her and her parents to visit her aunt. Later we decided to go to the movie. While looking for a seat, Betty noticed Barbara and Pat Grimes sitting with some other kids.*

*Outside the show we all got to talking and we exchanged phone numbers. When we got to the street where we turned off, we said good-by and ran across the street. Then Betty forgot something she had to tell Barbara and we ran back to the corner.*

*A man of about 22 or 25 was talking to them. He pushed Barbara into the backseat of a car and Pat in the front seat. We got part of the license number as the car drove by us. The first four numbers were 2184. Betty thinks there were three or four numbers after that. We didn't think so much about it but it struck us as kind of funny. When we heard that they were missing we didn't know what to do.*

The letter was unsigned and was never verified as having been written by an actual eyewitness. The police tried to check on the partial license plate that was provided, but it led them nowhere.

Some even came to believe that the letter might have been written by the man who abducted the girls, his motives as baffling as the fate of the Grimes sisters. Whoever wrote the letter, though, it was just one of the many strange objects, events, and people who complicated the investigation.

On January 10, a switchboard operator for the Catholic Youth Organization named Henrietta Marshall received a telephone call that not only sent chills down her spine, but promoted a police search of hundreds of automobiles in the Illinois Central Railroad's 12th Street Station and Grant Park parking lots. The caller on the other end of the line (which sounded like a young man, she later said) told Miss Marshall, "For God's sake, I need help! I need to talk to a priest!" When she told him that there was no priest available, he asked her if she knew the location of the Grant Station's parking lot. Henrietta said that she did not. "Well, I've got a thirteen year-old girl tied up in the trunk of my car there," the caller told her and then abruptly hung up. But the police found no one at the reported site - dead or alive.

On January 17, another report came in, this time from a woman named Pearl Neville, a traveler who was making her way by bus from Nashville, Tennessee, to her home in St. Paul, Minnesota. During a stopover at the Chicago Greyhound Bus Station, at Randolph and Clark Streets, she noticed a newspaper story about the two missing sisters. When she saw their photos, she believed them to be two "tired, bedraggled" girls that she had met in a Nashville restroom on January 9. She said that she had spoken to the girls briefly and they had said they were on their way to a state employment agency to look for work. A clerk at the agency claimed to remember the girls and to recognize them from their pictures. They had applied there under the name "Grimes," she said. Unfortunately, records were not kept for transient applicants, but the police were encouraged by the fact that the clerk remembered their faces. In Chicago, Pearl Neville met with Loretta Grimes, who reacted to the other woman's claims with both disbelief and hope. She still could not accept the fact that the girls had run away, but prayed they were still alive. The Nashville police were contacted about the alleged sighting of the two lost girls, but once again, their investigation led nowhere.

For Loretta Grimes, the New Year was ushered in by more false leads and dashed hopes. While the rest of the world was celebrating the start of the New Year, Mrs. Grimes kept a quiet vigil in the living room of her small, two-story house, unable to eat or sleep, only able to worry. New sightings continued to be reported, each bringing hope and then disillusionment and pain as they turned out to be untrue.

And before the girls' bodies were eventually discovered, things became really strange.

On January 12, Mrs. Grimes made a trip to Milwaukee, escorted by FBI agents, after she received three letters that demanded $1,000 for the safe return of her daughters. Daniel Fults, agent in charge of the

*Loretta Grimes in a posed newspaper photograph, looking at one of the information flyers that were handed out in hopes of finding the missing girls.*

Milwaukee office, said that the letters told her to go to three places in the downtown area -- a department store, hotel, and a Catholic Church. She was instructed to go to all three places at 11:00 a.m. and then again at 11:00 p.m. and then wait at the church with the ransom money on the bench beside her. The letters promised that Barbara Grimes would walk in to retrieve the money and then leave to deliver it to the kidnapper. She and her sister would then be released. No one ever came and Loretta was left sitting for hours to contemplate her daughters' fate. The letters were later traced back to a mental patient at the Veteran's Administration Hospital in Lake County, Illinois.

Sadly, by the time of Mrs. Grimes' fruitless trip, it's likely that the bodies of the two girls were already lying along German Church Road, covered with snow.

31

But if that's true, how can we explain the two telephone calls that were received by Wallace and Ann Tollstan on January 14? Their daughter, Sandra, was a classmate of Patricia Grimes at the St. Maurice School and they received the two calls around midnight. The first call jolted Mr. Tollstan out of his sleep but when he picked up the receiver, the person on the other end of the line did not speak. He waited a few moments and then hung up. About fifteen minutes later, the phone rang again and this time, Ann Tollstan answered it. The voice on the other end of the line asked, "Is that you, Sandra? Is Sandra there?" But before Mrs. Tollstan could bring her daughter to the phone, the caller had clicked off the line. Ann Tollstan was convinced that the frightened voice on the telephone had belonged to Patricia Grimes.

*Alleged psychic Walter Kranz, who told police that he dreamed the girls' bodies would be at what turned out to be a short distance from where they were discovered.*

And that wasn't the only strange happening to mark the period when the girls were missing. On January 15, a police switchboard operator, Ann Dorigan, received a call from a man who refused to identify himself but who insisted that "those two missing girls" were dead and could be found in Santa Fe Park at 91st Street and Wolf Road. He claimed that this revelation had come to him in a dream and he hung up. The call was traced to Green's Liquor Market on South Halsted and the caller was discovered to be Walter Kranz, a fifty-three-year-old steamfitter. He was taken into custody after the bodies were found on January 22 - less than a mile from the park that Kranz said he dreamed of. He became one of the numerous people who were questioned by the police and then released.

And he was far from the only one. Police Sergeant Ernest Spiotto reportedly questioned a young man arrested for cutting off a lock of hair from the girl sitting in front of him in a movie theater. This was only about a week after the Grimes sisters had vanished. The young man, like Walter Kranz, claimed to be a psychic and told Spiotto about a dream involving the two girls. Spiotto later said, "He told us that he had this dream about a field of trees and a tiny creek. He said there were two naked bodies there - bodies that looked like mannequins lying in the field."

Mannequins were exactly what Leonard Prescott thought he had seen as he was driving along German Church Road on January 22 - many days after the young man's arrest. Spiotto pulled the young man in for more questioning after the bodies were found, but he had a solid alibi and was released.

The two "psychics" were among what turned out to be the first of hundreds of suspects and so-called witnesses that were questioned by the police. Tragically, detectives are still waiting for the one clue that will solve this now very cold case.

# LOST GIRLS SLAIN

The search for the Grimes sisters ended on January 22, 1957, when Leonard Prescott spotted what appeared to be two discarded clothing store mannequins lying next to a guardrail, a short distance from the road. A few feet away, the ground dropped off to Devil's Creek below. Unsure of what he had seen, Prescott nervously brought his wife to the spot, and then they drove to the local police station. His wife, Marie Prescott, was so upset by the sight of the bodies that she had to be carried back to their car.

Once investigators realized the "mannequins" were actually bodies, they soon discovered they were the Grimes sisters. Law enforcement officials converged on the scene. The officials in charge, Cook County Sheriff Joseph D. Lohman and Harry Glos, an aggressive investigator for Coroner Walter E. McCarron, surmised that the bodies had been lying there for several days, perhaps as far back as January 9. This had been the date of the last heavy snowfall and the frigid temperatures that followed the storm had preserved the bodies to a state that resembled how they looked at the moment of death. As the newspapers broke the story on the morning of January 23, both the press and the investigators in the case began to draw connections between the murders of the Grimes sisters and Schuessler-Peterson murders, which had occurred under similar circumstances in October 1955.

Those murders had sent the region into a panic and the horror felt by parents in the Chicago area was only compounded by the disappearance of the Grimes sisters and the subsequent discovery of their bodies. Like the Schuesslers and Bobby Peterson, the girls had been found naked and dumped in a secluded, wooded area. Like the murders less than two years before (still unsolved at the time), the bodies were first mistaken for mannequins by those who had discovered them.

Sheriff Lohman was technically the lead official of the investigation. Square-shouldered, full-featured and normally possessing an easy-going smile, he immediately took charge of the scene - which would soon become chaos. Lohman was, by all

*Detectives at the crime scene on German Church Road. This newspaper photograph shows the bodies of the two girls in the spot where they had been dumped along the road.*

accounts, a decent man. He was an academic, though, with aspirations for the governor's mansion and no real experience with police work. He was totally out of his element in the Grimes case, just as he had been with the Schuessler-Peterson case the previous year.

Joseph Grimes was brought to the scene, dressed in his work clothes and flanked by two policemen. The two officers had met him at Bozzy Cartage Company to tell him about the discovery and to ask him to look at the bodies. His face turned pale at the news that his daughters might be dead and the officers offered him more time to prepare for the worst possibility. But Mr. Grimes agreed to accompany them to German Church Road. When he arrived at the site where the bodies had been dumped, he looked down at the pale naked bodies and began to cry. "Yes, they are my daughters," he choked and slumped over. One of the policemen, his own eyes

*Just as it had been at Robinson Woods in October 1955, police officers from various jurisdictions flooded the scene, trampling any evidence that would have been found along the road.*

clouded with tears, supported Grimes as they walked back to the nearby road.

The discovery of the bodies - along with their positive identification as the Grimes sisters - sent the various police departments into action. A short time after they were found, more than 160 officers from Chicago, Cook County, the Forest Preserves and five south suburban police departments began combing the woods - and tramping all over whatever evidence may have been there. Between the officers, the reporters, the medical examiners, and everyone else, the investigation was already botched. Despite the claims of Lt. Joseph Morris, the head of a special police unit investigating the Schuessler-Peterson murders, who said, "We're not going to repeat some of the mistakes that we made the last time," things were already off to a bad start.

*Police officers and volunteers search the area around German Church Road, hoping the killer of the Grimes sisters left a clue behind.*

Understandably, the police initially linked the murder of the two girls to the Schuessler-Peterson murders of the previous year. Sheriff Lohman was quick to point out for reporters all of the similarities between the murders, not the least of which that the nude bodies of the victims had been found in remote locations. He also noted that the bodies overlapped, as if they had been dumped or tossed from a car or truck. The bodies had been stripped in both cases and the clothing taken away (the clothing was never found in either case). The bodies all bore signs of violence and a cursory examination of the sisters showed similar wounds to those found on the murdered boys.

A search of the scene found a rusty beer can, a metal pipe-cleaning tool and a reamer, like a pipe smoker would use, and child's toy sheriff's set. The set, mounted on cardboard, included a large key ring with two jailer's keys, and a toy sheriff's badge. They were sent to the police laboratory for further analysis, but any link that they might have had to the murders has never been discovered.

The area around the bridge was roped off until it could be examined by crime scene experts, but the damage was already done. Investigators blamed failure to secure the Robinson Woods area from curiosity-seekers for the obliteration of possible valuable clues in the earlier case, but the police had destroyed most of the clues themselves. In the Grimes case, using the forensic standards of the day, there was no way to tell whose footprints, marks, and signs had been left behind at the scene. The site had been overrun within hours and by then, most clues had been lost.

The investigation became even more confusing in the days to come. The bodies were removed from the scene and were taken to the Cook County Morgue, where they would be stored until thawed out and an autopsy could be performed. Before they were removed,

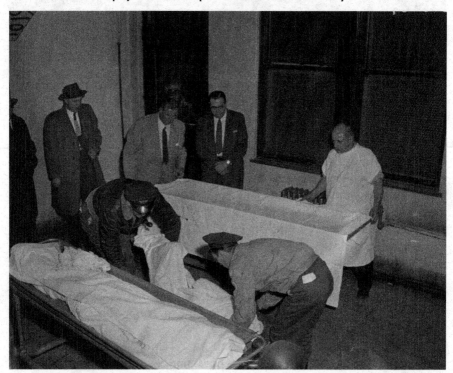

*The bodies of the Grimes sisters arrive at the Cook County Morgue, where more mysteries in the case would develop.*

however, both police investigators and reporters commented on the condition of the corpses, noting bruises, and marks that have still not been adequately explained to this day. According to a newspaper article, there were three "ugly" wounds in Patricia's abdomen and the left side of her face had been battered, resulting in a possibly broken nose. Barbara's face and head had also been bruised and there were punctures from what may have been an ice pick in her chest. Once the bodies were moved, investigators stayed on the scene to search for clothing and clues, but neither was found.

The autopsies were performed the following day, but all hopes that the examinations would provide new evidence or leads were quickly dashed. Despite the efforts of three experienced pathologists, they could not reach agreement on a time or even a cause of death. They stated that the girls had died from shock and exposure, but were only able to reach this conclusion by eliminating other causes. And by also concluding that the girls had died on December 28, the night they had disappeared, they created more mysteries than they had managed to solve. If the girls had died on the night they had gone missing, then how could the sightings that took place after that date be explained? And if the bodies had been exposed to the elements since that time, then why hadn't anyone else seen them? There had been several snowstorms that had come through the area, then melted, followed by another storm, in the time the girls had been missing. German Church Road was a remote location, but it still saw enough traffic that the bodies would have been noticed if they had been there the entire time.

Things were going to become even more confusing in the days and weeks that followed.

Meanwhile, shock was setting in at the Grimes home on South Damen Avenue. Friends, neighbors and clergy members gathered to offer solace and support for the family. Most found it hard to believe that the Grimes could lose two more children. Joseph and Loretta's second oldest child, Leona, who had married and left home, had died in August 1954 at the age of twenty-six. She had died at Holy Cross Hospital after a kidney operation. The family had all been at her side when she passed away. It was a terrible day - but nothing like what they were facing now with the disappearance and subsequent murders of two more daughters.

*Sister, Theresa, and mother, Loretta Grimes, after learning the shocking news that the bodies of the two girls had been found along German Church Road.*

After Barbara and Patricia had disappeared, Loretta feared she would lose them and began to blame herself for their disappearance. One day while the girls were missing, she appeared at the St. Maurice convent and after bursting into tears, told one of the nuns that she never should have allowed them to leave the house that night. If she had not let them go, the girls would be safe.

On Tuesday, January 22, her worst fears were realized when the police called her to tell her that the bodies of two unidentified girls had been found on German Church Road. At that point, they were not sure that they were the Grimes sisters. But Loretta was sure - she was already convinced that the dead girls were her daughters. She began to cry, insisting that the police had never believed her when she told them that Barbara and Patricia had not run away. If they had listened, she said, the girls might have been found. In a haze, she began repeating that she needed to go to church and rushed out the door toward St. Maurice.

Outside, her longtime friend and neighbor, Mrs. Joseph Kozak, intercepted her and led her to the Kozak house, which was located just two doors down. Mrs. Kozak then called Father Schomburg from St. Maurice, who immediately came and took Loretta back home. They arrived just in time for the awful confirmation that Joseph Grimes brought from the death site in Willow Springs. "It was them," he said softly, unleashing a fresh torrent of tears.

The afternoon dailies caught the story before they went to press, but the real headlines in the *Chicago Daily Tribune* and the *Chicago Sun-Times* came the following morning. Glaring bold words, "FIND 2 LOST GIRLS SLAIN!" capped articles and photographs of the two smiling, sweet-faced girls and their weeping family members. Joseph Grimes had been photographed immediately after identifying his daughters, being led from the scene by a kind officer with his face in a tearful grimace. Loretta, shown with her fists clenched, was crying and looked devastated. She was quoted as saying that she wished her life could be taken and her daughters be allowed to live.

Newspaper reporters went to the girls' schools, noting that students heard the news at St. Maurice in stunned, eerie silence. The principal, Sister Ritella, who had known both girls, described them as average students who were totally devoted to their mother and their home. Teachers at Kelly High, where Barbara attended, expressed the same shock and sadness.

The reporters also contacted Dorothy Peterson and Eleanor Schuessler Kujawa, the mothers of the three boys murdered the year before, to get their reactions. Dorothy Peterson said that she was almost too shocked to comment. She finally said, "I'm just so taken aback. I really can't say anything. It's just terrible. Part of your heart is gone... I know how Mrs. Grimes must feel and I know God will watch over her."

Mrs. Kujawa, who had recently remarried after the death of her first husband, Anton, who died just one month after the murders of their two sons, sent Mrs. Grimes a sympathy card with a personal message - "My heart goes out to you, Mrs. Grimes, for I know the terrible experience you have been through. Only a mother knows the worst, and although I hoped for the best, I, too, knew the day the children disappeared, that I would never again see them alive. Have courage in God and pray the killers of your daughters will be brought to justice."

The widespread sympathy for the bereaved family was almost overwhelming. Neighbors brought food to the Grimes home and people sent cards and letters, usually containing donations to help with their living expenses as Loretta had not worked since the girls had disappeared. Strangers went out of their way to try and help. A man that Loretta didn't know brought her $2, claiming that he had planned to use it to go bowling but wanted her to have it instead. A group of teenage girls from the neighborhood rang doorbells and asked for donations, raising $253 for the family. Local schoolchildren gathered donations from friends, teachers and family members. A neighbor brought $25 to the Grimes house, impressed that fourteen

*The Back of the Yards Neighborhood Council set up a fund for the Grimes family and enough money was eventually collected to allow Mrs. Grimes to pay off the mortgage on her home.*

year-old Joey had shoveled her sidewalk every day, including on the Tuesday that he learned of his sister's deaths.

The Back of the Yards Neighborhood Council set up a fund and received donations in the mail, varying in amounts from 50-cent pieces to a check for $500. The council started a fund drive, led by retired police captain Matthew Murphy and Father Schomburg from St. Maurice. Mrs. Grimes used some of the money from the fund to buy clothes for herself and the children to attend the sisters' funeral service, which was conducted free of charge by the Wollschlager Funeral Home. St. Maurice Church provided the gravesites for the two girls. Eventually, the fund received so much money that Loretta was able to pay of the $7,726.25 mortgage on her home.

But all of the money in the world wouldn't bring her daughters back.

*A boy prays in front of the closed caskets of Barbara and Patricia Grimes. The funeral brought thousands of people to St. Maurice for the services.*

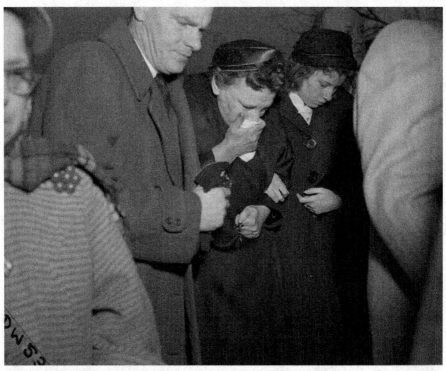

*A grieving Loretta Grimes, accompanied by Theresa, at the funeral of her two daughters.*

The wake for the sisters started on Friday, January 25 and on Saturday, it seemed that half of Chicago showed up. A nun from St. Maurice said that she came out of the door of the convent and saw people lined up all the way from the entrance to the funeral home to Archer Avenue. Not all of them came to express their sympathy and sadness - there were plenty of morbid curiosity-seekers in the crowd - but nearly everyone was outraged and grief-stricken by the sight of the two closed caskets with photographs on top resting in that small funeral home.

The Grimes case had, if possible, become even more galvanizing to the people of Chicago. Residents, especially parents, were still unsettled by the Schuessler-Peterson murders. They had searched, prayed and hoped for a happy ending to the disappearance of the two girls and now were shocked all over again by their murders. Panic about the safety of children gripped the region. Parents were terrified, keeping their youngsters inside and close in ways that they had never done before.

Many felt compelled to try and help the police solve the crime. The Back of the Yards Neighborhood Council sent out letters to area residents, offering a $1,000 reward for information leading to a conviction in the case and outlined the ways that the public could help the authorities. Friends Danielle Blotteaux and Barbara Drzewiecki, both seventeen, who matched Barbara and Patricia in size and height, posed in clothing duplicating what they wore on the night they disappeared. The photographs were published in the newspapers with hope that they would jog the memory of anyone who might have seen them - and lead the authorities to their killers.

The funeral for Barbara and Patricia was held on January 28. By this time, the hysteria about the murders had reached a fever pitch. Classmate Rosemarie Rancatore was an acquaintance of Barbara's and was asked to serve as a pallbearer. She described the funeral as a "three-ring circus" that nearly made her sick. "The press was the worst," she later said, "stepping all over headstones, plants and flowers. It was awful."

However, it soon became evident that the reporters were not the worst. The deaths of the two girls brought out the best in most people, inspiring acts of charity and kindness, but in others, it encouraged the dark side of human nature. Someone, after seeing the names and addresses of the pallbearers in the newspaper, began warning their parents over the telephone that they, too, would never see their daughters again. The young ladies who had been asked to be pallbearers had to be taken home early from school. Dorothy Weinert, one of the pallbearers, said that her mother had gotten a call from someone who told her, "Your daughter's next." Police officers drove her home from the cemetery after the funeral.

Barbara and Patricia were laid to rest at Holy Sepulchre Cemetery in Worth one month after they disappeared - their mystery no closer to being solved than it had been in December.

# BUILDING A
# MYSTERY

Despite the best intentions of everyone involved in the investigation of the Grimes sisters' murders, the case was seriously flawed from the start. Efforts were being made to find the killer, but he was eluding them. Investigators questioned an unbelievable 300,000 persons, searching for information about the girls, and 2,000 of these people were seriously interrogated, which in those days could be brutal.

The biggest problems were coming from all of the confusion in the case. With all of the different police jurisdictions involved, no one could agree on anything. And since it was Chicago, everything seemed to be driven by political rivalries and personality clashes. These problems managed to hamper the investigation, which was further compromised by the destruction of clues by careless reporters and photographers who were anxious to get their stories into print.

Even the medical professionals couldn't agree on anything. An assumption had been made that the girls had been lying on the side of the road since the night they had disappeared. If that was true, why had no one seen them?

Elizabeth Lundeen, who lived in LaGrange, told police that she had driven on German Church Road to a friend's house around noon on January 22, an hour before Leonard Prescott discovered the bodies. She had driven slowly, she said, because of the snowy conditions and passed right by the spot on the bridge. "I'm sure the bodies weren't there then," she insisted. American Airlines pilot P. Marvin Althaus, who lived nearby on German Church Road, drove across the bridge at 8:30 a.m. and he agreed that the bodies had not been there.

However, a couple who lived nearby, Mr. and Mrs. Peter Wootos, told a different story. According to their account, their Great Dane was awake and whimpering throughout the night of January 21. The next morning, he was determined to run across the road to the bridge, something he had never done before. They were sure that something strange had occurred on the bridge during the night. If the bodies had been dumped in the darkness, why had no one seen them during the morning hours?

Yet another account suggested that the girls had been there much earlier, perhaps, as some officials claimed, as far back as the night they disappeared. Earl Kirkpatrick, a forty-year-old truck driver from Decatur, Illinois, worked for Dohrn Transfer Co. in Cicero and he believed that he had seen the Grimes sisters on the night of December 28, less than four miles from where their bodies were discovered on January 22. He placed the time at 11:30 p.m. and said one of the girls -- the taller one, which would have been Patricia -- was wearing only a blouse and panties.

"They were in the full glare of my headlights," Kirkpatrick said, "and I saw them clearly."

He told police that his truck was loaded with merchandise and he was driving to Sheffield. His initial thought when he saw the young women on the side of the dark highway was that they had been placed there as decoys by hijackers who wanted him to stop so that they could rob him.

"They didn't hail me or turn to look at me," he said. "They were just walking along through the snow. It was very cold."

Kirkpatrick's report tied in to some investigator's theories that the girls were taken out into the country by teenage boys on the night that they went to the movies.

"I hadn't paid much attention to the Grimes case, but my wife got the idea this week  he came forward in mid-February 1957  that the girls I saw may have been the two sisters, so I decided to come to the police," he later told reporters.

Unfortunately, Kirkpatrick's sighting could never be corroborated and no one could ever be sure if it was the Grimes sisters that he saw, or someone else entirely.

Officials - and the general public - hoped that answers would be revealed by the autopsies. Investigators hoped that they might jumpstart the foundering investigation. Coroner Walter McCarron was attending the inauguration of President Eisenhower in Washington, D.C., and so, in his absence, his assistant, Harry Glos, was in charge of assigning the procedures. Glos demanded to be present, as a representative of law enforcement agencies, during the five-hour examination performed by three esteemed pathologists -

Drs. Augustus Webb of the coroner's staff, Edwin F. Hirsch of St. Luke's Hospital, who was in charge of the examination of the vital organs, and Jerry J. Kearns, chief pathologist of St. Elizabeth's Hospital and a former pathologist from the coroner's office. Dr. Walter J.R. Camp, considered one of the top toxicologists in the country at the time, tested the blood and tissue samples taken from the bodies.

But, to the surprise of everyone involved, the initial results from the autopsies offered no new leads and little information. Dr. Kearns referred to the postmortem examinations as "one of the roughest cases I've seen during my many years in the coroner's office."

In the end, the only cause of death that they could come up with for the two girls was secondary shock resulting from exposures to temperatures that reduced body temperatures to below the critical level compatible with life - in other words, they froze to death. They had reached this decision by eliminating definite causes like shooting, stabbing, strangling, or poisoning. The puncture wounds and marks on the girls' bodies, they determined, occurred after death and were not serious enough to have been fatal. Dr. Kearns stated that the murderer was "diabolically clever" and used a method - perhaps a mysterious poison - that they could not detect.

Although he wasn't "diabolically clever," one of the first real suspects in the case was the alleged psychic, Walter Kranz, who was mentioned earlier. He had called the police on January 15 and claimed the girls could be found dead in Santa Fe Park. Once the bodies were discovered just a short distance away, the police took a deeper interest. Kranz was arrested and brought in for questioning. The newspapers called Kranz "an enigma." He was held at the Englewood station for observation, questioned and given lie detector tests about his "dream" and his telephone call to the police.

According to records at the Chicago & Northwestern Railway, where the lanky, soft-spoken, six-foot-five oddball had worked since June 1956, Kranz had been absent from his job four times between December 28 and his arrest. Kranz blamed his absences on his wife being sick. He was given a glowing reference by his boss, who described him as a good worker who knew his trade. Kranz claimed that his "vision" had simply come to him after a night of drinking. He swore he had no connection to the murders. "My soul is clear," he said.

The police also questioned Kranz about a letter that had been sent to Mrs. Grimes before the girls' bodies were found. The letter had demanded $5,000 be left in a locker at the LaSalle Street rail station to secure the Grimes sisters' release. Handwriting experts were almost certain that Kranz had written the letter, but he refused to admit it and no evidence could be found to tie him to it. He was eventually released, dismissed as another crank with a macabre interest in the case.

In the midst of the initial start of a murder investigation, the autopsies and the questioning of Walter Kranz, the police also had to deal with scores of other nuts and crackpots, would-be amateur detectives, more so-called psychic visions, and a number of false confessions, which made their work even harder. One confession that they investigated came from a transient who was believed to have been involved in some other murders around the same time period. His confession later unraveled and he admitted that he had lied.

By Thursday, January 24, eager to crack the puzzling case, Sheriff Lohman ordered the arrest of a new suspect in the case, a Skid Row dishwasher named Edward L. "Benny" Bedwell. The arrest of the drifter, who sported Elvis-style sideburns and a ducktail haircut, would mark the beginning of an investigative debacle that would confuse, confound, and anger the public and cause even greater grief to the beleaguered Grimes family.

# FROM MCKINLEY PARK TO SKID ROW

Chicago's "Skid Row," a name once given by major cities to areas of town where the unemployed, transients, and drifters frequented saloons, gambling houses, and dilapidated hotels, was located on the city's Near West Side. From the onset of the Great Depression until the late 1980s, the area centered on Madison Street, loosely reaching from Lake Street to Van Buren and Clinton west to Damen. It was largely an unchecked haven for alcoholism, poverty, crime, and down-and-outers from all walks of life. In its heyday, a walk down Madison Street meant wading through a sea of garbage and broken glass and stepping over at least twenty men sleeping on the sidewalk or passed out in the gutter. The West Loop, as it's better known now, was an area of boarded up businesses, flophouses, dive hotels, drunks, bars, and burlesque houses. The area has changed tremendously in recent years, but in 1957, Skid Row was at its peak - or perhaps at its lowest point; a better description. Skid Row was a long, long way from the safe streets of McKinley Park, which made the idea of two Catholic girls from that southwest side neighborhood spending time there impossible for the public to believe and unbearable for their family to consider.

But that's exactly what was being said about Barbara and Patricia Grimes.

A cab driver named Reno Echols, in response to photographs that he saw in the newspaper, came forward and told the police that he had seen the Grimes sisters on the morning of December 30 in the D & L Restaurant, located at 1340 West Madison Street - the heart of Skid Row. Echols, who lived less than a block away from the diner, insisted that the girls were there at 5:00 a.m. with two men. He didn't recognize one of the men, but the other, with sideburns like Elvis Presley, had been around the place before. He was sure the girls with them had been the Grimes sisters and added that they looked "sick, or drugged, or drunk."

*Skid Row on West Madison Street in 1957*

His story was corroborated by the restaurant's elderly owners, John and Minnie Duros. They both identified the two girls as the slain sisters and said the man with the sideburns was a customer who sometimes washed dishes in exchange for food. According to the account of Minnie Duros, the group had entered the diner early in the morning on December 30. She said that two teenage girls, one taller than the other, entered the restaurant with the dishwasher and another man and sat down in a booth. She said that the taller girl was either so drunk or so sick that she was staggering as she walked. She was "in bad shape," Mrs. Duros noted.

The couples sat in a booth for a while, listened to Elvis songs on the jukebox, and then went outside. According to Minnie Duros, "The taller girl returned to the booth and put her head on the table. They wanted her to get into the car, but she didn't want to. The other girl and the two men came back later and I told them to leave the girl alone -- she's sick. But they all left anyway and on their way out, Barbara said they were sisters."

Mrs. Duros was distracted by customers, one of whom was Reno Echols, in the front part of the restaurant and while she waited on them, the man she identified as Bennie Bedwell dragged the seated girl out the back door, while the other girl protested.

According to Mrs. Duros, the group returned later that morning and it appeared that Barbara had paired off with the would-be Elvis lookalike, Bennie Bedwell. She said that they were carrying on, so

*The D & L Restaurant (Left) on Skid Row around the time of the alleged sightings of the Grimes Sisters with Bennie Bedwell. The Harold Club entrance is in the center, a location where Bedwell allegedly also went with the girls.*

she asked them to leave. Bedwell paid the bill and left. A few days later, he came back into the restaurant and Mrs. Duros asked him what had happened to the girls. By this time, she had seen the news reports and realized who the two young women were.

Bedwell told the old woman that he had the girls. Mrs. Duros allegedly warned him," You'd better send those girls back home because the police are searching for them. It'll be your neck if they catch you with them." Duros said that Bedwell hung his head and walked out of the place.

Minnie Duros would not be the only one who claimed to see the Grimes sisters on Madison Street on December 30. Willie Jackson, a resident of Paulina Street, saw two girls walking with a man near Madison and Western Streets at 3:30 a.m. Vito Martinez said that he saw the Grimes sisters a half hour later at Madison Street and California Avenue. Another witness believed that he saw them around 9:00 p.m. that evening. Walter Scott told police that he had seen them at 3:00 a.m. at Madison Street and Ogden Avenue and then at the D & L Restaurant later that morning.

But the story began to unravel... Minnie Duros was called into Monroe Street police station to speak to the detectives there about some issues with her story. Duros seemed to be unsure about the date of the alleged visit by the Grimes sisters to the D & L. She was unsure if it had been December 30, as she originally stated, or January 6, one week later. The newspapers eventually began reporting the date of the visit as January 6, which still poses problems with the theory that the girls had been dead - and lying on the side of German Church Road - since December 28.

Detectives also wanted to know why Duros had waited so long to report seeing the girls and the two young men with them. Police had searched Skid Row after the girls had disappeared and detectives Sidney Rubin and Henry Ulrich had stopped into the D & L to speak to the owners. Duros claimed she had not been questioned at the time, but the detectives distinctly remembered her telling them that she was not interested in getting involved in the affairs of her patrons.

Duros' account was as shaky as her memory, but the police were interested in the part-time dishwasher, Bennie Bedwell. They tracked him down at the Star-Garter Theater, located at 815 West Madison Street, a former burlesque house that now opened at 8:00 a.m. and

*An ad for shows at the Star and Garter, where Bedwell was arrested -- not exactly one of Chicago's more reputable theaters.*

showed double feature movies throughout the day and evening. He was arrested there by sheriff's detectives who refused to tell reporters anything about him, only that his name was "Bennie." The sheriff's office confirmed his arrest but refused to say anything more. Chicago police immediately complained that they were not informed of the arrest and said that it violated a "pledge of cooperation among the various law enforcement agencies." In other words, it was "business as usual" with the Grimes case.

But the Chicago police didn't have to wait long for details. They could read all about the arrest in the newspapers on January 24. Once the story broke, the name Bennie Bedwell became known all over Chicago.

Edward Lee Bedwell, known by his childhood nickname of "Bennie," was a tall southern boy with long, Elvis-style sideburns and a slicked back, ducktail haircut. Born in March 1935 (or 1936, depending on the document he produced), in Graves County, Kentucky, his family moved to Paris, Tennessee, when he was a young child. He grew up in this country town in the central part of the state and at age eighteen, he went to work for the Ringling Brothers and Barnum & Bailey Circus in Sarasota, Florida. His time with this reputable show was a short one and he was soon working as a roustabout for a carnival based out of Deland. At some point before he drifted to Chicago, he was arrested for vagrancy in Las Vegas, Nevada.

Once in Chicago, Bedwell signed up for the U.S. Air Force at a local recruiting station. He only served for six months. There are conflicting stories about his discharge. One claimed that his hands were too sensitive because of burns that he suffered from a hot stove when he was a year old. Another version involved the fracture of his kneecap, reportedly sustained in a laundry room brawl during this stint in the Air Force. In another account, both incidents occurred - he fell and injured his kneecap but couldn't use crutches because of his hands. He was released from the service in April 1955.

Bedwell was just twenty or twenty-one years old when he was arrested for questioning in the Grimes case. He'd been living at the McCoy Hotel, a Skid Row flophouse, located at 949 West Madison Street. He'd been drawn to the area by family connections.

His mother, Ethel Lee Barnes, was just 16 when she became the fifth wife of John Edward Bedwell, 30 years her senior, in November 1929. They were divorced in 1951 based on grounds that he "willfully

*The McCoy Hotel, a once fine establishment turned Skid Row flophouse, where Bedwell was living at the time of his arrest in the Grimes case.*

and maliciously deserted her," and during the last years of their marriage, "took to strong drink." Ethel later remarried and with her new husband, Curtis Bradberry, lived at several addresses on Chicago's Near West Side, starting in 1951. By the time that her son was arrested for questioning about the two murders, she and her husband and daughter, Shirley, lived in a three-room apartment at 1430 West Monroe Street.

Ethel, just over five feet tall and weighing more than 200 pounds, retained her Tennessee drawl as she described her son to reporters as a lazy boy who thought the world owed him a living. Bennie had been living with her and his stepfather in November 1956, borrowing small amounts of cash and stealing cigarettes until Ethel kicked him out. But even so, he could not have committed murder. "He's a good

*The Century Theater on West Madison where Bedwell took two girls he claimed where not the Grimes Sisters, but who ditched him when they went to the restroom. He initially told police that he never saw them again.*

boy," she said. "I'd like to go and see him. If he did anything wrong, I know he'd tell his mother."

But he didn't. In fact, Bedwell claimed that he'd never met the Grimes sisters. He admitted that he had been with two girls at the D & L, but they were not the two missing girls. The taller girl, who witnesses identified as Patricia, told Bedwell that her name was Carol - or so Bedwell claimed. He further explained that, while they all attended a movie at the Century Theater at 1421 West Madison Street, the girls went to the restroom and ditched him and the other man by slipping past them in the lobby and exiting onto the street. "That's the last I saw of either of them," he said, stating again that they were not the Grimes sisters.

By the time that the police caught up with the second man at the D & L, Richard Whittemire, Sheriff Lohman considered Bedwell the prime suspect in the case. Whittemire, 28, confirmed going to the D & L with Bedwell in late December, but without the girls that witnesses claimed were with them. He said that he wasn't sure of the date and that there had been another man with them who had a dark complexion and was probably a Puerto Rican.

Whittemire, short and skinny, had a long police record, dating back to his juvenile delinquent days in his hometown of Mansfield, Ohio. He was charged with parole violation in 1951, and in June 1955, was charged in Jonesboro, Arkansas, with grand larceny after stealing two watches worth $81. In June of that same year, he was arrested again for "willfully and feloniously" abandoning his pregnant wife, Sadie Belle. He spent time in jail and later drifted to Chicago. By the early days of 1957, he was living at the Balboa Hotel, a flophouse in Cicero.

Whittemire said that Bedwell was a "ladies man," but he denied getting involved with any girls with him on Madison Street. During his questioning by police, two girls came forward to corroborate Bedwell's story. Irene Dean, nineteen, from Grand Rapids, Michigan, told police that she and her cousin, Carol King, eighteen, had been the two girls who accompanied Bedwell and the other man to the D & L Restaurant. She claimed that her cousin paired off with the second man, around December 29 or 30, while Dean had been Bedwell's date. Mrs. Duros, when questioned about this turn of events, said she remembered seeing Irene Dean at the restaurant at other times, but never with Bedwell. She stated once again that she was sure the girls who came in with Bedwell were the Grimes sisters.

And almost as soon as these two women come forward, possibly clearing the dishwasher of suspicion, he made his first confession -- not that he had killed the Grimes sisters, but that the two girls had not been Irene Dean and her cousin, but Barbara and Patricia Grimes. It had been the Grimes sisters that he'd been seen with at the restaurant after all, he was now telling detectives.

According to Bedwell's new statement, he'd met Barbara and Patricia, along with a man that was already in their company, at 7:30 or 8:00 p.m. on December 29, at the Harold Club, located on West Madison, next door to the D & L Restaurant. He offered the "biggest one" a drink and she had accepted, but when they ordered drinks for all four of them, the bartender refused to serve the girls because they were too young. They left the bar and went to another place a few doors down, the Green Front Tavern. They had six or eight rounds of drinks, went to the D & L for food, and then returned to the Green Front for more drinking. At their next stop, another bar on Madison Street that Bedwell could not remember the name of,

*Another view of Skid Row on West Madison. The Star and Garter Theater is on the right.*

they were told by the bartender that he wasn't going to serve them. They'd had enough. After that, they went to Ralph's Club, drank some more, and then went on to the theater, where the girls supposedly ditched the two men after going to the restroom. Bedwell insisted that he didn't know that they were the two missing sisters at the time.

His story went on from there. In contrast to his earlier statement about never seeing the girls again, he now claimed that he had seen the Grimes sisters several times during the next few days. After their night of drinking, he ran into them in various places in the area, including the Jackpot Tavern, located in the 900 block of West Madison. He claimed that he had seen the "taller one" there alone on two occasions and saw them both together a couple of other times.

At the same time that Bedwell was locked up and spinning a new yarn, the police were receiving information about a whole batch of new sightings. A few hours before Bedwell claimed that the two girls in his story were the Grimes sisters, a woman named Mario Scaperdine, who lived on West 51st Street, told police that she had seen two men, Bedwell and a curly-haired second man, with the Grimes sisters on the afternoon of December 29, the day after they disappeared. She identified Bedwell and the two girls from photographs and said that she had seen them in front of a store in the 1900 block of West 51st Street. She had noticed them because the two girls looked dazed. She said that she saw a ballerina slipper on the curb across the street from her home the next day. Despite the chilly night, both girls had worn ballerina-type shoes to the Brighton Theater on December 28.

Grace Kritikos, the manager of the New Albany Hotel at 231 South Halsted Street (Greektown, and just two blocks off Skid Row) claimed that she refused to rent a room to Bedwell, two girls, and a dark-complexioned man on the night that Barbara and Patricia disappeared. She said that the girls were too young. After the bodies were found and the story broke wide, she contacted the police and told them about the incident, positively identifying Bedwell and the two girls from photographs.

Ann Povich, a waitress at Mount Pindos Restaurant, located at 4950 South Pulaski Road, claimed that Bedwell was there with another man and two girls at 7:30 p.m. on December 28. She said that the girls had ice cream sundaes and then they left with the two

*A 1980s-era photograph of the Mount Pindos Restaurant on South Pulaski Road, where a waitress reported seeing Bedwell with the Grimes sisters.*

men, Bedwell and a stocky, dark-haired man in a pea coat. Although she identified the girls as the Grimes sisters - and even said that one of them called the other "Petey," which was Patricia's nickname - she might have been mistaken. The girls had left home that night at 7:15 p.m. and were later seen at the Brighton Theater. However, the restaurant was less than two miles down Archer Avenue from the theater. It's possible that they could have been picked up near their home by Bedwell and the other man, driven to the restaurant, and still have easily made it to the movies. Ann Povich was insistent that this is what happened. She was adamant that the Grimes sisters had been there and, years later, before her death, still found the experience too disturbing to discuss at length. She often said, "I tried to help the police back when the whole thing happened and they wouldn't listen to me."

A man named Leonard Wass claimed to see the sisters in early January. He said that Barbara and Patricia and two men (one a sailor - or perhaps just wearing a pea coat?) came into the service station that he operated at 45th Street and Archer. He remembered

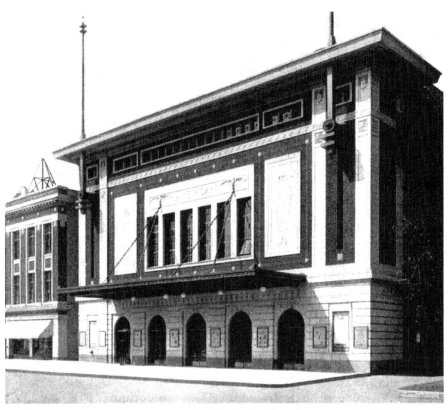

*The American Theatre at 8 North Ashland, just off Skid Row,*
*where the Grimes sisters were reportedly seen between*
*January 5 and January 10.*

that the girls asked to use the restroom and, as they were leaving, the one he identified as Barbara gave him a "strange look," which he interpreted as her desire not to get back into the car.

Edward Martel, night clerk at a hotel at 1521 West Warren Boulevard (just a block off West Madison Street), identified Barbara Grimes as a girl he saw leaving a restaurant at 1520 West Madison on January 5. Robert Hilpertshauser, manager of the American Theater at 8 North Ashland Avenue (just north of Madison), said he saw the girls there on various days between January 5 and January 10.

Casey Jarzen, owner of the Sunny Lane drive-in restaurant at 5444 Harlem Avenue (just off Archer Avenue, near Summit, Illinois),

*The Sunny Lane Diner in Summit, where the Grimes sisters were reported with Bedwell on January 11.*

agreed with his wife, Mary, his daughter, Donna, and their cook, Chester Wiziecki, when they told police that Bedwell, and a second, dark-complexioned man, were in the restaurant on January 11 with two girls they identified as Barbara and Patricia. Wiziecki told the police that one of the girls wore a black jacket with the name "Pat" embroidered on the left collar. The sheriff's department said that Loretta Grimes stated that Patricia was wearing such a sweater on the night that she and Barbara went to the movies.

A pawnshop clerk named Edward Frankel reported that he saw Patricia Grimes in his shop at 950 West Madison Street in early January. She came in hoping to pawn a watch. He told police that he wouldn't take it, though, because she was too young. He recalled the encounter after seeing a newspaper photo of the watch that Barbara was wearing when the girls disappeared. "It was a Bulova of a design you don't see very often," he told detectives. "I remember it well."

Both detectives and the general public were puzzled about the new sightings. They had occurred after the girls had vanished and when some officials thought they were already dead. In addition, what had they been doing on Skid Row - hanging out in bars, cheap hotels, and theaters? Were the sightings real, or was someone mistaking two other girls for the Grimes sisters?

Before investigators had a chance to puzzle out what was going on, Bedwell came up with yet another story. He told detectives that he had actually witnessed the murders of Patricia and Barbara at the hands of "Frank and Louie," two men who were partying with the girls on January 13. Bedwell said that "Frank" was fair-complexioned and "Louie" was dark, possibly a Puerto Rican. Both men were in their twenties. He joined the two men and the Grimes sisters at a few taverns on Skid Row and then the entire party went for a drive into the southwestern part of Cook County. After stopping at a gas station at 87th Street and Archer Avenue, where the girls used the restroom, they drove to the entrance of a forest preserve with a hilly incline and parked the car. Bedwell said that he sat in the front drinking while the two couples made out in the backseat. He soon heard scuffling and turned around to see that the two girls were dead.

One of the men said that they needed to do something with the bodies - and that everyone had better be quiet about what had happened. The two men stripped the bodies, he said, and dumped them on the side of the road. After driving him back to his hotel, Bedwell never saw the two men again.

Officers decided to check out the story, driving Bedwell out to the Southwest Side so that he could re-trace his steps that night. No one at the service station recognized him, or photos of the girls, but Bedwell took them to the forest preserve with the hilly area that he described. He seemed confused when he got there. When one of the detectives asked him what the problem was, he replied that he had made up the entire story. When asked why he would do that, Bedwell replied, "I thought you'd let me go if I told you."

As Bedwell was being taken back to the car, headed back to a holding cell, he changed his mind again and came up with a third version of his confession. This time, he offered a full-fledged

*Bedwell re-enacting how he claimed that he had dumped the bodies of the Grimes sisters on German Church Road. Bedwell is next to the railing, Sheriff Lohman is next to him.*

admission of guilt, replacing the "Louie" character in his story with himself. He and "Frank," he admitted, took the girls to German Church Road on January 13. He and "Frank" beat them and then dumped them nude and unconscious in a snowbank. He claimed that they stopped for hot dogs at the Sunny Lane Restaurant, on South Harlem Avenue, on the way. The beating, according to Bedwell's account, followed a seven-day binge during which he and the other men took the girls to liquor and sex parties in cheap taverns and hotels on Skid Row.

Bedwell was forced to reenact their movements on that night again. He was accompanied by Sheriff Lohman himself, surrounded by police detectives and uniformed officers, reporters and a crowd of curiosity-seekers who heard about what was going on. According to Bedwell, they had taken the girls to the forest preserve and he and his supposed accomplice had each punched one of the two victims, rendered them unconscious, and left them lying in the snow because the girls had refused to have sex with them.

Along the way, he pointed out the drive-in restaurant and a service station that he said he, "Frank," and the two girls visited. According to his statement, they traveled the remote roads in bitter cold weather and wound up near the Willow Springs Woods. The girls resisted their advances and he and the other man got angry, beat the girls, and then "got scared" when they found the girls were unconscious. They stripped the girls at Frank's suggestion "to get rid of fingerprints." Bedwell carried Barbara and Patricia from the car and tossed them in the snowbank. The two men then fled back to the city and separated, with Frank saying that he would get rid of the girls' clothing.

When Bedwell, Sheriff Lohman, and their assorted entourage reached the spot on German Church Road where the bodies were found, Bedwell looked around, seemingly confused. He hesitated and then said, "Yeah, this is the place. I hit Patricia on the chin and I knocked her out. And how Frank knocked her Barbara out, I don't know." He shook his head and looked at Sheriff Lohman. "I didn't mean to hit her so hard." Bedwell said that he hadn't believed the girls were dead when the two men drove away. He was sorry for the Grimes family and blamed his bad behavior on his childhood. "If I had a decent break at home and got an education, I wouldn't have been a bum around flophouses."

Sheriff Lohman was convinced by the story. He found the whole thing plausible, thanks to the identifications of various people who had seen Bedwell with the girls and also because of Bedwell's resemblance to Elvis. Lohman believed this might have been enough to get the girls to go along with him. And then, of course, there was Bedwell's confession - all three of them. Unfortunately, the stories not only contradicted each other, but they failed to explain many of the facts, like the puncture wounds on their bodies and the absence of other critical signs of violence.

Everyone doubted the veracity of the confession but Lohman, which is odd considering that he had been quoted in the newspaper as saying, "He is definitely not telling the truth. He lied on so many points I can't enumerate them. He contradicts himself repeatedly."

As soon as the reports of Bedwell's confession reached the newspapers, reporters immediately began pointing out the flaws in the story. They were skeptical, as was the Grimes family. Loretta Grimes, who was preparing for her daughter's funeral, cried, "It's a lie! It's a lie!" when she was told of Bedwell's confession. She added, "My daughters wouldn't go to Madison Street. They didn't know where it was."

Reporters also noted the lack of an explanation for the puncture wounds that were found in Barbara's chest, which were thought to have occurred after her death. They also questioned Bedwell's story that they had stopped for hot dogs at the Sunny Lane diner on the way to Willow Springs. This supposedly occurred just before they were killed and yet the autopsy report showed that the stomachs of the girls were empty. One thing not noted, though, was that the owners of the diner, their daughter, and their cook, also gave the date of January 11 as the day they saw the Grimes sisters in their restaurant. Bedwell claimed the trip had taken place on January 13.

But the main thing that the reporters clung to when they pointed out the flaws in the confession was that Bedwell claimed to have had sexual relation with Patricia Grimes. According to the autopsy report, though, both Patricia and Barbara were without sexual experience - - or at least that's what it said. It would later turn out that the autopsy report did not contain all of the facts.

Flawed or not, Sheriff Lohman accepted Bedwell's confession and he booked the drifter and dishwasher on murder charges. The public, willing to believe what the authorities said, breathed a sigh of relief when they heard that the Grimes sisters' killer was behind bars.

But he would not stay there for long.

# THE CASE UNRAVELS

Ethel Bradberry, Bedwell's mother, never paid much attention to her son until he got into trouble. After he was held in jail for five days, she went looking for a lawyer. While many inmates have not fared well over the years with court appointed attorneys, Bedwell got lucky. David E. Bradshaw was an up-and-coming Chicago lawyer who belonged to the Defense of Prisoners Committee, a small group of private attorneys selected by judges to represent certain clients pro bono. Bradshaw was an aggressive, hard-headed young lawyer who would prove to be a thorn in the side of the determined Cook County Sheriff.

After meeting with his client, Bradshaw made a statement about his disgust with the fact that Bedwell had been without an attorney for five days. He told reporters, "The boy in this case is wholly illiterate, doesn't understand what is going on, and has found himself the main object in a case of nationwide interest." Bradshaw also dismissed the Grimes sisters as "two young girls from a good South Side family, suddenly popping up on a wild spree on Skid Row." He maintained that this was what his client was being punished for, and that he was a convenient scapegoat for girls who got themselves into trouble. He pointed his finger at Lohman and the investigative team for what he called their "unusual treatment" of Bedwell, who had never been offered an attorney. He suggested that the sheriff had conducted certain tests on Bedwell and that the results of the tests should be released.

No one involved with the case - save for Sheriff Lohman - was surprised when it started coming apart.

In the days that followed Bedwell's third bizarre confession, Lohman managed to find Bedwell's partner in crime, William Cole Willingham, Jr. He was being held at the House of Corrections on a drunk and disorderly charge, and at first, his statements seemed to add credence to Bedwell's story. Offering to take a lie detector test, Willingham admitted that he had been on a drinking spree with Bedwell and two young women. However, he insisted that they were Irene Dean and her cousin, Carol King, not the Grimes sisters. When

Carol King was shown photos of Bedwell and Willingham, she identified them as the two men she and her cousin had met on West Madison Street and ditched at the Century Theater.

Willingham, born in Washington, D.C., was raised in Virginia and had spent most of his life in trouble with the police. He said that he had last seen Bedwell on January 5, the day they were carousing on Skid Row with the cousins from Michigan. He was arrested later that same day for being drunk and disorderly and was released on January 6. Willingham claimed that between January 10 and January 12, he had worked at the Stineway Drug Store at 4761 North Broadway. On the day that he allegedly went with Bedwell to German Church Road, January 13, Willingham claimed that he spent most of the day around the Wilson Avenue and Broadway area, where he borrowed $1 from the manager of the Stineway Drug Store and left an I.O.U. behind. That evening, he went bar hopping and then visited a friend at 619 North Dearborn Street. Fred Pratt, the manager at the drug store, confirmed that Willingham had worked there and that he had indeed borrowed $1. It didn't seem that the young man had been anywhere with Bedwell on the day that Bedwell claimed the girls had been killed, but other witnesses confused the issue.

Minnie Duros, after seeing Willingham's photo, insisted that he had been the man who was with Bedwell and the Grimes sisters at the D & L Restaurant. Chester Wiziecki, cook at the Sunny Lane where Bedwell allegedly stopped for hot dogs with the girls on January 13, was unable to pick Willingham out of a group of inmates. Oddly, though, Willingham denied that his nickname was "Frank," but inmates at the House of Correction stated that he had indeed been called "Frank" while inside because he liked to sing and imitate Frank Sinatra. To make matters more puzzling, police found a date book that Willingham had been carrying, which listed more than fifty female names. At the bottom of one page was a lone entry - "Grimes." But Willingham claimed that it was a customer from his part-time job selling premium certificates for a photography studio.

On January 30, Coroner Walter McCarron began the first of three inquest proceedings into the deaths of the Grimes sisters. It was a contentious affair and the bickering that occurred really characterized the entire investigation. The various jurisdictions had fought over the case for more than a week, and now, Bedwell's attorney David Bradshaw was added to the mix of battling officials.

McCarron started the proceedings with a ridiculous statement that implied that all of the law enforcement agencies involved with the investigation had cooperated with one another. After that, he called his first witness: Loretta Grimes. The small, quiet woman was not accustomed to speaking publicly and yet she felt compelled to serve as a

*Coroner Walter McCarron*

spokeswoman for the morality of her girls. She was angry and upset about Bedwell's claims that her daughters had been drinking and engaging in sex on Skid Row. Equipped with eleven pointed questions and her own determination, she was an impressive force that the various officials had to deal with. Like so many people in the McKinley Park neighborhood, she refused to believe what was being said about her daughters. The rumors had gotten so bad that the pastor at St. Maurice had been forced to address the congregation from the pulpit, admonishing them for spreading stories about Barbara and Patricia.

Shortly after McCarron began to question her, David Bradshaw stood up and moved closer to the front of the room. Investigator Harry Glos pointedly told him to sit down. Bradshaw explained that he was trying to hear the testimony, suggesting that Glos mind his own business. The exchange got McCarron's attention and he addressed Bradshaw, telling him that he wanted to be fair to him since he was an attorney representing one of the people involved.

Bradshaw feigned shock. "One of the people involved? I am the attorney of record for Edward Lee Bedwell!"

McCarron assured him that he had a right to hear everything and Bradshaw told him that this was why he was moving closer, so that he could hear everything. But Harry Glos felt different. He was sure that Bradshaw was moving closer to try and intimidate the witness.

"We have no secrets," McCarron replied and went on with questioning Mrs. Grimes about the girls' last meal on December 28. Bradshaw interrupted twice to say that he couldn't hear and had McCarron repeat her last answers. He then informed McCarron that he had questions of his own to ask the witness, to which McCarron demanded to know what they were. Bradshaw said that he would rather ask them directly. McCarron was becoming upset. He was intent on protecting Loretta from Bradshaw, even though she shared the attorney's desire to clear Bedwell, even if it was for different reasons. Finally, McCarron snapped, "You want to hurt her some more? Go ahead!"

Bradshaw barked back. "I'm not here to hurt anyone. I am here to defend the rights of the boy."

Eventually, Bradshaw was granted his request and asked Mrs. Grimes her opinion about the stories that placed the girls on West Madison Street and about the guilt of Bennie Bedwell. He asked, "Mrs. Grimes, as you sit here now, do you believe that Edward Lee Bedwell, who is here in this courtroom today, was involved in this occurrence with your daughters?" The question drew objections from both the coroner and Assistant State's Attorney Robert J. Cooney. They insisted that the question was unfair and that there was no way for Mrs. Grimes to know who killed her daughter.

In the midst of the bickering between the officials, Mrs. Grimes managed to croak out the word "no" in reply to Bradshaw's question. She later told reporters that she believed Bedwell's confession was a "pack of lies." Bradshaw also asked Theresa Grimes, the murdered girls' older sister, if she believed Bedwell's "alleged and purported" confession. She answered with an emphatic "no."

This set off a new round of arguments between Bradshaw, Cooney and Coroner's deputy C.F. Dore, who wanted Bradshaw's questions - and their replies - stricken from the record. The bickering continued - and grew worse. Bradshaw engaged in a three-way fight when he questioned Sheriff Lohman about the location of Bedwell's confession. He knew that Bedwell had been taken to the Southwest Side to reenact the alleged crimes when he confessed a third time. Lohman replied that it had occurred at "a motel known as Caprello's at the corner of 55th and Cicero." Bradshaw knew that the owner of the hotel had Chicago gangland connections, so he was trying to embarrass the sheriff by asking. Cooney insisted that the question was irrelevant and Lohman managed to dodge it. The three men went back and forth for some time before the session was finally closed.

The fighting continued during the final session on February 11. Bradshaw, McCarron, and Cooney continued to spar and then things got a little strange when the sisters' friend, Dorothy Weinert, took the witness stand. Dorothy was asked about her meeting Barbara and Patricia at the Brighton Theater on December 28. Dorothy said that she had seen the girls each buy a box of popcorn and a candy bar and after this innocent statement, Loretta Grimes jumped out of her seat and shouted at the horrified young woman, "Liar! You're a liar!"

She insisted that not only did they not eat popcorn as Dorothy claimed, but that Dorothy didn't see them at the theater at all. The popcorn issues created a discrepancy in the amount of money that the girls had with them to spend. Mrs. Grimes reiterated that she had given them $2.50, but 50 cents for the bus ride home, $1.50 for admission to the theater for both girls, and 50 cents for two boxes of popcorn, added up to $2.50. But Dorothy claimed they had each bought a candy bar, spending another 30-cents they supposedly didn't have. Where had this money come from? No one could say and, strangely, if Dorothy was lying and never saw the girls that night, then perhaps the sisters never went to the movies at all, which meant that maybe they were on Skid Row with Bennie Bedwell as he claimed. That was obviously something that Mrs. Grimes did not want to consider.

Dorothy was not the only witness that Mrs. Grimes upset that day. Leonard Prescott was called on to testify and he became defensive when Bradshaw asked him about the position of the girls' bodies. He quickly assured the attorney that he had not touched them, even though Bradshaw never said that he had. When Prescott refused to answer one of Bradshaw's questions, Bradshaw asked Cooney to direct him to do so. Cooney said that Prescott didn't have to answer, that photographs from the police department clearly showed the positioning of the bodies. Bradshaw countered that Captain Fleming was not the witness he was questioning. Prescott never answered the question and the photographs showing the exact positions of the bodies were never introduced.

To his relief, Prescott was dismissed, but he and his wife became upset and insulted when they saw Mrs. Grimes rolling her eyes about his testimony and remarking, "Boy, that one's a character."

Marie Prescott was particularly upset about the incident. "We were trying to help and after all we were going through, we felt that she didn't have any reason to say a nasty thing like that about my husband."

When Mrs. Prescott mentioned "all we were going through," she was referring to the intrusion of the police into their daily lives. Their discovery of the girls' bodies had thrust them into the public spotlight and had even made Leonard Prescott the object of suspicion to some of the investigators in the case. Since January 22, officers had shown up at their home at all hours of the day and night and had questioned them and searched the house several times. "It was like they believed we had done something," Marie said.

Loretta Grimes was upset over the entire inquest, and specifically about the things that were being said about her daughters in the newspapers and through neighborhood gossip. She challenged just about everything that Bedwell said, especially that he had engaged in sex with Patricia. She believed that science supported this belief - - but she was wrong.

As far as Mrs. Grimes and newspaper reporters knew, examinations of the girls' bodies showed no trace of sexual abuse. In addition, the autopsy stated that neither of the girls were sexually experienced. When reporters asked Dr. Edwin Hirsch, a pathologist, for a "yes" or "no" answer on the question of whether or not the girls had been violated, the doctor demurred. He replied that the question involved morals rather than science. He finally said, "The question you are asking is, 'Are they chaste?'"

The pathologist couldn't answer the question because he was under strict instructions not to do so.

But Mrs. Grimes had an answer for them. In front of a battery of microphones, television cameras, and the press, she tearfully insisted, "Our girls came from a good home and were brought up in religious surroundings. Now our children are dead and cannot deny these lies

72

but our family has to live with them. We demand an absolute vindication until proved otherwise."

She went on to demand answers from the reporters, asking how Bedwell could have signed his name to hotel registers with the girls when he was illiterate and how he could have taken them into saloons when they were just young girls. She stated: "Our girls looked like children and did not look fully mature and physically developed for their age. How could they be taken by saloon keepers as adults? Would a tavern owner risk his license selling liquor to children?"

Mrs. Grimes refused to believe it. "My daughters were good girls," she stated adamantly.

But the truth was, Bedwell did live in one of the seedy hotels on Skid Row, where he had signed the register. He was mostly illiterate, but he was able to sign his name and he could read, although at an elementary school level. As far as the tavern owners on Skid Row went, they would sell liquor to just about anyone. If a person was brave enough to cross their doorway, they were, on almost every occasion, willing to sell them a drink. West Madison Street was home to the dregs of Chicago at that time and no one was worrying much about licenses and drinking ages. Any tavern owner questioned by the police was quick to say that he would never serve alcohol to an underage drinker, but the truth of the matter was that no one on Skid Row really cared, as long as the drinks were paid for.

And it got worse from there. What few people knew at the time was that portions of the autopsy reports had not yet been released to the public. When what was contained in the reports was finally leaked, there were serious repercussions for the case. By then, though, it was too late.

It wasn't long before Bedwell's vague and contradictory confession would be recanted, likely on advice of his attorney. He quickly claimed that it had been beaten out of him. He said that he had confessed out of fear of Lohman's men, who had struck and threatened him while he was being questioned.

According to his new version of events (his fourth), Bedwell denied ever seeing the Grimes sisters. His entire fourteen-page confession, he said, was a lie.

Around this same time, a toxicology report was released, claiming that the girls had died on December 28 -- the night they had disappeared -- which not only made Bedwell's confession untrue, but also refuted a lot of reliable eyewitness testimony that placed the girls on Madison Street and on the Southwest Side for two weeks after they disappeared.

In the report, it stated that there was no sign of alcohol in the girl's systems, which meant that they could not have been drinking on West Madison for days prior to their deaths. It also said that an examination of Barbara's stomach turned up particles of fish and potatoes, the last meal the girls had eaten at home before going to the movies. But, bizarrely, even though Patricia had eaten the same meal, nothing had been found in her stomach.

The report had a disastrous effect on the inquest and on the case against Bennie Bedwell. Unfortunately, it was likely incorrect. A short time later, the report -- as well as others from the autopsy -- would be sharply criticized by one of the principals in the case. But, as stated already, it was too late by then to keep Bedwell behind bars.

The report invalidated the confession from Bedwell, which had already retracted before Chief Justice Wilbert F. Crowley in criminal court. During a hearing that started on January 30, and ended the following day, Bedwell said that he had confessed because the police had beaten him and then alternated between scaring him and bribing him. He'd been slapped, kicked in the shins, and punched in the mouth, causing his lips to bleed. His main attacker was Chief Clifford J. Dreyer, who punched him in the ear and threatened to bring a blackjack to the interrogation room to get some straight answers from him. Bedwell also implicated a sergeant at the Bedford Park Sheriff's police station who forced him to strip to his underwear and threatened to take him out to German Church Road, where he'd be forced to stand in the snow until he confessed. After his first confession, officers had given him cigarette money and offered to treat him well if he would "be nice and tell the truth."

Despite the number of witnesses who placed Bedwell with the Grimes sisters, he now claimed that he had never met them. He had concocted the story after hearing his co-workers at the Elegant Bakery, a bread shop in the McCoy Hotel building at 949 West Madison where he had lived and worked for a time, talking about the Grimes sisters' disappearance. Bedwell said that he had seen pictures of the bridge on German Church Road in the newspaper, which is how he found the place. He told reporters: "I had seen pictures of the dead bodies and of the scene and I also had the story read to me by a woman in a restaurant and I remembered parts of the story and I made it up, fitting myself into it."

Sheriff Lohman, still convinced that Bedwell was guilty, denied the charges of abuse. He also maintained that Bedwell had lied to Judge Crowley on the witness stand. He still considered Bedwell to be the lead suspect in the case, "even more so now than when we took his first confession."

During the hearing, Assistant States Attorney Cooney questioned Bedwell about his charges of brutality and the drifter continued to claim that he had been beaten by detectives. Lohman's police staff followed him to the stand and, not surprisingly, they denied every claim that Bedwell made.

But Bradshaw, Bedwell's attorney, managed to make the detectives look bad on the stand, questioning their investigative techniques and their pursuit of Bedwell. Bradshaw also managed to track down witnesses to help his client. James Powers, a supervisor at the Ajax Consolidated Company where Bedwell worked for about a month, produced time cards that showed Bedwell had punched in at 4:19 p.m. on December 28, and punched out at 12:30 a.m. on December 29, which covered the window of time when the girls had disappeared. A co-worker at Ajax came forward and validated the alibi.

The case against Bedwell was rapidly falling apart, but he found his accommodations in jail were better than his rundown flophouse on Madison Street. Kept in isolation at the request of his attorney, he had music piped into his cell and dined on food that was much better than he could afford on his own. Monetary offers poured in from magazine and television shows, all anxious to "get the real story." A theatrical agent even approached him to try and learn to sing and play guitar so that Bedwell could go on tour as "the next Elvis." Locally, Bedwell had a minor following, with people writing to Bradshaw about how they donated clothing to the indigent prisoner. Some sent small amounts of money, eventually totaling about $150. None of his fans or would-be agents, though, were anxious to come up with the $20,000 bond money that was required to set him free.

Even after his confession had been tossed out by the judge, Bennie Bedwell managed to keep his warm bed in jail for a little while longer -- as the search for the Grimes sisters' killer returned to the neighborhood where the girls had grown up.

# CLOSER TO HOME

As the case against Bedwell began to collapse, police investigators returned to the neighborhood between the Grimes house and the Brighton Theater to look for more clues.

Lieutenant James McMahon of the Brighton Park police district told reporters: "There is no doubt in our minds that the answer to the Grimes mystery lies right in the area of the girls' home. They disappeared in that area. Either they were kidnapped there or willingly got into the car of someone they knew. Either way, the trail starts there."

Witnesses from the area provided information that indicated the girls had left the Brighton that night, went on foot down Archer Avenue and almost made it home.

One witness was Roger L. Menard, who lived with his parents at 3825 South California Avenue, near Kelly High School. He had been at the showing of *Love Me Tender* on December 28, and had sat behind the Grimes sisters

*The grief-stricken Loretta Grimes sits on the curb outside her home in the McKinley Park neighborhood, perhaps waiting in vain for answers to the mystery of her daughters' deaths.*

77

and Dorothy and Jeannette Weinert. The girls had left the theater about one minute after he did and they walked behind him as he proceeded down Archer Avenue. He could hear them talking and laughing as they walked along after him. Just as they were passing Fishman's Liquors, two doors east of Sacramento Avenue, he heard the squeal of brakes and turned around to see a late model green Buick pulling up to the curb next to the girls. The car came to a stop, its motor racing, and the two girls hesitated for a moment, almost as if they knew who was in the car, or maybe they were surprised that the car had stopped at all. There was a slight hesitation and then the car pulled away. Menard said that the girls kept walking.

Just past 42nd Street, he stopped to look into the window of Lewis Men's Wear and when he started walking again, Barbara and Patricia were ahead of him. A second car, a black Mercury, this one occupied by two teenage boys, pulled up. The boy on the passenger side rolled down his window and said something to the girls. Menard wasn't close enough to hear what was said, but the girls looked at

*A 1949 Mercury, like the one described by Roger Menard. This make of automobile was very popular with young men in the 1950s because it was easily customized into a "hot rod." Menard mentioned that the car he saw on the night the girls disappeared may have been fitted with a sunshield over the front window.*

each other and giggled. They kept on walking and the car pulled away.

Menard was sure about the make of the car. He said that it was a 1949 model because it was a model that a lot of teenagers bought because it was easily customized. The car was a four-door, jet black, and in excellent condition, Menard said. There may have been a sunshield on it, also black, over the front windshield. Menard couldn't tell the police anything about the boys in the car, except that one was tall and the other seemed to be short because he was low in the seat.

Two other young men, Earl Zastro, 15, and Ed Lorden, 17, were riding around that night and saw the girls as they were walking home. The two friends knew the Grimes sisters, not personally, but by sight. At around 11:25 p.m., they noticed the girls walking on 35th Street between Seeley and Damen Avenues. The boys said that they were giggling and jumping out of doorways at each other. Curious as to who they were, the two boys drove around the block for a better look. "Oh yeah," they said to each other, "It's those two Grimes sisters."

A few days later, on December 30, Zastro mentioned the sighting to a police officer who was questioning customers at Angelo's Restaurant, but nothing came of it at the time. That changed in February when investigators renewed their interest in the neighborhood as the case against Bedwell was unraveling. The boys were both taken out of school several times and questioned - and threatened - by the police.

Earl Zastro lived with his parents above their grocery store at 3833 South Wolcott Avenue and the police actually accused him of killing the girls and hiding their bodies in the store's freezer. He later joined the Air Force and was home on leave in the summer of 1959, when the police resumed their interest in him again. He was followed and questioned, but after going overseas for three years, this seemed to bring their suspicions to an end.

While Bedwell was spending his final days in jail, the investigation on the Southwest Side continued. New leads, both in McKinley Park and near the body dump site, made headlines and then seemed to go nowhere.

One lead came from a man named Robert Mitchell, who owned and operated a diner and filling station at Joliet and Willow Springs

Roads. He said that he had arrived at his station to open for business on the morning of January 19 to find a twenty-something man requesting a push for a stalled car. Mitchell helped him out and drove him to German Church Road in his tow truck. A second man of about the same age was waiting at the stalled car, a 1956 medium green, two-door Ford hardtop with elaborate bumper guards. The car had broken down about four miles from the spot where Patricia and Barbara were found a few days later.

Mitchell saw a section of gray cloth, which might have been a blanket or a coat, hanging out of the Ford's trunk and he asked the second man why he hadn't used it to stay warm while he waited. Mitchell told police, "They gave me a none-of-your-business look. I was alone, so I didn't press the matter." Barbara Grimes had been wearing a coat of that same color when she left home on December 28. Mitchell was sure that neither of the men had been Bennie Bedwell.

Unfortunately, Mitchell had no idea who the men were, had not taken note of their license plate number, and had no idea where they had gone when he left them. It was an interesting story, but there was no way for the police to trace the two men.

Sheriff's police officers discovered hair and what appeared to be human flesh inside of a cardboard box in the snow along German Church Road, just west of County Line Road. It was on farm property that belonged to Emmett Keller. The hair was wrapped in newspapers dated September and November 1956. The police lab eventually determined that neither the flesh nor the hair belonged to the Grimes sisters - but who it might have belonged to was never discovered.

Police found a message printed with chalk across the wooden support on the back of a shack located near the site. It was on land that belonged to Carl Rink, who lived in Clarendon Hills. The words "HELP HELP B & B HELP HELP," were interspersed with one arrow pointing upwards and one pointing downwards. The letters "L" and "P" in the first word were printed backwards. Lieutenant David Purtell, a handwriting analyst, was brought in to compare the writing on the board to the word "ELVIS" that had been written on a stove in a gas station at 37th Street and Damen Avenue. According to the station attendant, it had been written there by one of the Grimes sisters. But Purtell said that the single word contained too few letters to make a definite comparison.

On February 2, new information was released by the police in hopes that it might spark new leads and perhaps gain more outside help in the search for the killers. Apparently, when the bodies of the two girls were discovered on January 22, the police also discovered an imported gold perfume atomizer and a gold eyebrow pencil near the bodies. They kept these two discoveries secret because some investigators theorized that what the newspapers called "beauty aids" could have been used to lure the sisters into a car on the night of their disappearance. If they could learn who had purchased the expensive items, it might lead detectives to the last person to see the girls alive. But the police search led nowhere, so Lieutenant Joseph Morris turned to reporters to get the word out about the atomizer and the eyebrow pencil. Anyone with knowledge about them was asked to come forward, but this avenue of investigation also turned out to be a dead end.

In and around the McKinley Park neighborhood, a squad of 33 policemen were sent on another canvass of every house, apartment, and place of business. Other units rounded up known gang members from the area, including four local toughs who were wanted for questioning in two beatings, several assaults, and for running a bowling alley employee out of the neighborhood. The first beating had occurred on December 24, when the four men had assaulted two brothers, Kenneth and Robert Lenkart. A third beating victim, Gerald Gierut, a sailor home on leave, told police that he had been viciously assaulted by the same four teenagers while walking through the park on December 29, the day after the Grimes sisters had disappeared. All three of the young men had been hospitalized with their injuries. The attacks had all occurred in the neighborhood where the Grimes family lived.

One of the gang members who was arrested was Richard Byrnes, who was sixteen. He had already been questioned by the police on December 31, while the girls were missing because he had reportedly been seen talking to them. Loretta Grimes also accused him of teasing the two girls the previous summer. Byrnes denied the allegations, but admitted that he knew Theresa Grimes, but said that he had not talked to her in months. He was given a lie detector test in late February 1957, but was cleared of having any first-hand knowledge of the murders.

One of his companions, Robert Darding, who was eighteen, said that he also knew Theresa. When questioned by the police, he stated that she had accused him of abducting her sisters on December 29, but swore that she was wrong. Both boys insisted that they had nothing to do with the girls' disappearance or their murders. The police uncovered several incidents of assault by the boys but could never connect them to the murders. All of them were given lie detector tests, but as far as investigators could tell, they were simply a handful of local toughs who, while violent, had nothing to do with the Grimes murders.

The police repeated their house-to-house canvass of McKinley Park. While it was going on, a truck driver named Daniel Eshelman came forward and reported seeing the girls on the night of December 28. Eshelman worked for the Standard Fuel and Furnace Oil Company and, while out making late deliveries, saw two girls resembling the Grimes sisters get into a dark-colored car with three men as they stopped in front of his truck at Archer and Western Avenues. Before they entered the car, he said, a young blond man of about twenty got out and spoke to them. One of the girls seemed to know the man, but the other stood back away from the car, as though she was reluctant to talk to him. The car went east on Archer Avenue and Eshelman soon lost sight of it. The sighting occurred around 10:45 on the night that the girls disappeared, but he never reported it, thinking that it wasn't important. He also reluctantly admitted that he'd failed to say anything because he was hoping that he would see the car again and get attention as the man who solved the crime.

On February 4, a dark-colored 1951 Mercury - which police hoped was the mystery car that kept turning up in witness statements - was found abandoned in McKinley Park. The car's owner, Charles Tirva, Jr., who had served time for burglary and contributing to the delinquency of a minor, turned himself in to the police when word of the abandoned car reached the newspapers. He was questioned and given a lie detector test, but he was found to have no knowledge of the murders.

It was obvious at this point that the police were grasping at straws, no matter how weird they turned out to be. Even possible sexual offenders were getting mixed up in the case. Joseph P. Dinsdale, twenty-seven, who was a truck driver and happened to own a 1949 Mercury four-door sedan, was accused by four girls from Kelly High School of indecent exposure in late January. The girls said that they were walking near 38th and Kedzie and he made improper suggestions to them and apparently exposed himself. Dinsdale was picked up and given a lie detector test to make sure that he had no connection to the Grimes sisters' murders.

Soon, the black Mercury was back on police radar again. Two brothers, Charles Bobb, twenty-five, and David Bobb, twenty, lived in McKinley Park and went to the Grimes home to report that they had been incarcerated in Georgia and while there, were told by a fellow prisoner that he was afraid that his car - a black Mercury, which he had abandoned in Detroit - might have been used to abduct the sisters. Meanwhile, Mrs. Grimes received a telephone call from a woman who claimed that she saw a black Mercury at Taylor and Halsted Streets occupied by two men with long sideburns.

On February 8, the mysterious Mercury turned up again in a new report. This one came from a car salesman named Stanley Zdziarski, who lived at 4002 South Archer Avenue. On the night of December 28, he was at home watching television in his upstairs apartment when he heard voices outside. He went downstairs to the front door and saw a car parked at the curb. The men in the car were talking to two girls standing on the sidewalk. Zdziarski was able to describe one of the men as about six feet tall, one-hundred-eighty pounds, with blond, bushy hair and wearing a beige Army jacket. One of the girls, he said, was dressed in a gray coat and had a kerchief tied over her head, similar to what Barbara Grimes was last reported wearing. His description of the car closely matched the one given to police by Roger Menard - a black 1949 or 1950 Mercury. He couldn't say whether the girls got into the car or kept walking, but he was sure about the date. He confirmed it by checking the *TV Guide* for the movie that he had been watching.

On the same day that this report emerged, police began searching for the writer of two letters that had been received at the Grimes home. One of them had arrived on February 7, and the first had shown up one week before. The letter writer implicated himself and someone named "Trudy" in the girls' murders and asked for forgiveness from Loretta Grimes. Why these letters seemed more convincing than the scores of other letters that Mrs. Grimes had received is unknown. She received letters of condolence, bizarre confessions, and enough death threats that the police began to provide protection outside of the Grimes home and officers accompanied the family members as they went about their daily routines.

Around this same time, two letters from different men (although both from Alabama) prompted Sheriff Lohman to secretly fly down to the southern state to question their writers. One man in Athens, Alabama, claimed to know Bennie Bedwell and had information about the murders. The second letter, mailed from Decatur, Alabama, mentioned a car that might have been used in the abduction. Neither lead amounted to anything worthwhile.

Another lead came from yet another truck driver who was out of town. He passed it on to a fellow driver, who told the police. The first trucker stated that he had seen two girls near 71st Street and Mannheim Road (less than three miles from the body dump site), walking in the dark during the early morning hours of December 29 - hours after the Grimes sisters disappeared. He was certain that the clothing the girls were wearing, which he saw in his headlights, was identical to that worn by Barbara and Patricia when they disappeared. He failed to report the sighting until the middle part of February because he was on the road and unaware that the murders had occurred. This was almost the same report that had been given to the police by truck driver Earl Kirkpatrick, except in that case, the girls had not been wearing clothes. However, just like the earlier report, this sighting also led nowhere.

Lead after lead was investigated, and then dismissed. The investigation was faltering and growing colder with each day that passed. As one week led into another, it became less and less likely that the case was going to be solved. Desperation was in the air.

In a very questionable move, the *Chicago Tribune* began soliciting opinions about the murders from their readers, paying $50 for each theory that they published. Letters poured into the newspaper offices, numbering into the thousands within days.

The theories ranged from the plausible to the outright bizarre. And as with the previous tips and leads given to the police, there was a wide range of people who wanted to be part of the investigation, from armchair detectives to nuts, cranks, and alleged psychics. The theories ran the gamut from those who believed the girls were killed on the night they disappeared and stored in a deep freezer until they could be dumped, to those who suggested they had wandered into an unheated building on their way home and had accidentally gotten locked inside, where they froze to death. The building's owner, terrified of being involved with the police, dumped the bodies. The letter writer suggested that the police check every unheated building on the Southwest Side for clues. Another writer suggested that the killer was the same man who killed the Schuessler-Peterson boys, which was not an uncommon theory at the time.

Another writer, D.C. Lewis, claimed to have no amateur detective abilities but suggested that perhaps the girls were picked up by someone, taken to an isolated spot, and then hypnotized into taking off their clothes. Something went wrong and he dumped the bodies on German Church Road. He wrote, "I would recommend a search be made among friends and acquaintances of the girls to find a boy, or boys, interested in hypnotism."

By this time, the public had largely dismissed Bennie Bedwell as a suspect in the crime, choosing to believe that his confession had been forced by the police. This ignored the numerous eyewitness accounts that put Bedwell with the girls at locations other than the D & L Restaurant, where he might have been with the two cousins from Michigan, as they claimed.

But Sheriff Lohman had not forgotten those witness accounts and he remained steadfast in the idea that Bedwell was involved in the case - and guilty of murder. In early February, he tried again to break Bedwell's alibi by holding Richard Whittemire, Bedwell's drinking buddy, in a West Side hotel for more questioning. Whittemire had worked with Bedwell at Ajax Consolidated, and at some point in the investigation, had reportedly signed a statement that Bedwell had not gone to work on the night on December 28 - no matter what the time clock said. Whittemire said that he was with Bedwell on West Madison Street on the night of the 28th and into the early morning hours of December 29.

The investigation continued to unravel and while it did, Bedwell was freed on $20,000 bail. Morris Brown, a bail bondsman from Champaign, Illinois, was looking to do Bedwell a good turn and also to get some free publicity. He took it upon himself to secure the bond money that Bedwell needed. When a building that he tried to offer as security was rejected as not being worth enough, he put in $500 of his own money and got the Summit Fidelity and Security Company to come up with the rest. To make sure that Bedwell didn't jump bail, Brown assigned his burly nephew, Monte Goleman, to follow him around and keep an eye on him.

Bedwell's release turned into an event. Unable to write his full name of Edward Lee Bedwell, he was allowed permission from the judge to sign out as "Bennie Bedwell," the only words that the illiterate drifter was able to scrawl. He signed out on February 5, and was whisked off by his attorney, David Bradshaw, to the luxurious Belden Stratford Hotel, where there would be a press conference later that day. The lawyer promised that his client was not going back to the flophouses and saloons.

# SECRETS THAT WENT TO THE GRAVE

The release of Bennie Bedwell from jail set off another round of bickering between police departments and various jurisdictions and the case became even more mired in red tape and inactivity. Things got even worse when coroner's investigator Harry Glos came forward and resurrected the problems with what officials considered to be the Grimes sisters' time of death. According to reports, they had died on December 28, soon after they had disappeared.

Harry Glos knew this wasn't true - as others likely did as well - but he was the only one talking about it. Glos, like Lohman, believed that Bennie Bedwell was somehow mixed up in the case. There were too many eyewitness reports of him with the girls that couldn't be easily dismissed and too many contradictions in Bedwell's various versions of what had occurred. Had he killed them? Glos didn't know, but he did know that the two sisters had not simply perished from cold while lying on the side of the road. At that point, the public was still unaware of just how violently the girls had been treated before they were killed. Their cause of death was much more complicated than officials had been admitting. Glos told newsmen, "There were marks of violence on those girls' faces. I know that. And the police know that, too."

Glos shocked the city with his announcement, but he was far from finished. The public had been lied to about the girls' deaths, even about when they had died. Science proved that Barbara and Patricia had not died on December 28, as the reports had originally claimed. Glos explained that an ice layer around the bodies proved that they were warm when they were left along German Church Road and that only after January 7 would there have been low enough temperatures, and enough snow, to create the ice and to hide the bodies.

Glos also raised the issues of the puncture wounds and bruises on the bodies, which had never been explained or explored. He also had plenty to say about the contents of the girls' stomachs, stating that he'd heard one of the doctors performing the autopsy say that curdled milk was found in Barbara's stomach, but this never appeared in the official report. Glos also noted the eyewitness accounts of the girls eating popcorn at the theater that night. If they had died on December 28, then why was there no popcorn in their stomach contents?

He was sure that the girls had been violently treated prior to death and also asserted tests proved that Patricia Grimes had been sexually molested before she was killed. Male sperm had been found in the vaginal fluid taken from her body. The pathologists had denied this, but the Chicago Police crime lab reluctantly confirmed it. However, they were angry with Glos for releasing the information because they wanted to keep it secret so that they could use it when questioning suspects. Chief of Detectives Patrick Deeley stated, "This kind of knocks the props out from under us. With this secret, which we had in our possession all the time, we were able to conduct a private search for a certain type of criminal."

The secrets had been revealed, but there was more that Glos didn't know and couldn't reveal. According to Lohman staff members who saw the autopsy slides, both girls were sexually assaulted before their deaths. This fact never appeared in the official reports and did not come out until many years later.

The coroner, Walter McCarron, promptly had Glos fired and many of the other investigators in the case accused him of being reckless and of political grandstanding. McCarron simply said that he was "publicity mad." Glos told reporters that his firing had been "politically motivated." He said that he was in trouble with his boss as far back as Christmas, "when my name was mentioned as a possible contender for sheriff." Glos, a former policeman and Republican precinct captain, said that McCarron, who was also a Republican, objected to his running for sheriff and told him, "You're not going to run." McCarron stated, however, that Glos was fired for not following orders and for releasing the information that the police had wanted kept quiet in the reports. As far as the problems with the various reports went, McCarron said that he was satisfied with the results that showed the girls had not been sexually active. The coroner dismissed Glos' claims by saying that Glos and the police technician upon whose findings Glos based his statement were not trained in medicine.

But time would prove McCarron to be wrong. Harry Glos, who died in 1994 and never gave up on the Grimes case, had evidence that the girls had been sexually active - and not just immediately before their deaths. He always believed that Coroner McCarron refused to release this information because of religious reasons or to spare additional grief for the family. Glos also went to his grave believing that Bennie Bedwell was mixed up in the case somehow.

He wasn't the only one who thought so. After Glos was fired, only Sheriff Lohman, who later deputized Glos to work on the case without pay, remained on his side. He agreed that the girls had likely been beaten and tortured by a sexual predator that lured them into the kidnap car under a seemingly innocent pretense. Lohman remained convinced until his death in 1969 that the predator who had killed the girls had been Bennie Bedwell. Other theories maintain that the girls may have indeed encountered Bedwell, or another "older man," and rumors circulated that the image of the two girls had been polished to cover up some very questionable behavior on their parts. It was said that they sometimes hung around a bar on Archer Avenue where men would buy them drinks. One of the men may have been Bennie Bedwell, some believed.

In the meantime, there were rumors of cover-ups and secrets surrounding the continuing police investigation in McKinley Park. As February 1957 was drawing to a close, the investigation was once again in the newspapers, as if the police were making one last-ditch effort to wrap things up. They were almost out of time, for the case had turned so cold that most feared there would be no solution to it. They pulled in several men known to be sexual deviants and those who had a history of molestation, questioned them all, and had to let all of them go free. It was a desperate move that gained no new information.

On February 22, newspapers reported that a babushka (head kerchief) discovered a week earlier where the sisters' bodies were found resembled one worn on the night they disappeared. The information had been kept from the public, pending laboratory tests - tests that led nowhere.

Two additional McKinley Park residents belatedly reported things that they had seen around the time of the sisters' disappearance. On February 28, Francis Suver, fifteen, reported seeing Barbara and Patricia followed by a black and red car on December 27, the night before they disappeared. William Absher, forty-six, told police that he had been taking a walk on the night of December 28, and saw Barbara and Patricia talking to three boys in a black and red car, which was parked at 35th and Damen Avenue. The time of the sighting coincided with their trip to the Brighton Theater. According to Absher, Barbara called one of the young men "Jack." He was the same man that called out to Barbara as she walked away, "You'll be sorry."

Joseph Riotta, who lived on South Tripp Avenue, reported to the police that he had seen two girls resembling Barbara and Patricia dragged into a car at Western and Archer on December 28. Once he made the report, he received a telephone call from a man who threatened to kill him if he talked to the police again. A police guard was assigned to his home.

People were starting to be careful about what they said. No one wanted to end up with police guards like the Grimes family and Joseph Riotta. Young men in the neighborhood had been threatened and harassed by police detectives, eager to track down any new leads. A few people made some disparaging remarks about the size of the relief fund that had been donated to the Grimes family, only to be intimidated from the pulpit at St. Maurice, where "thoughtless parties" were told to remedy the situation with a few words of kindness. Those "words of kindness" extended to the Grimes sisters themselves. Rumors had started to spread that Barbara and Patricia were not as innocent as their mother wanted everyone to believe. Those who spread the rumors were also denounced by religious leaders in the community.

Then came a surprise from Delores Castillo, fifteen, who shared a locker with Barbara Grimes at Kelly High School. She came forward to report that Barbara had once shown her a picture of her boyfriend and that she referred to him as "Eddie." Delores, having seen photos of Bennie Bedwell in the newspaper, believed that he was the same man. Barbara said that she had met Eddie, who she described as a "hillbilly" from Wisconsin who drove a Buick, in September 1955 at a local five and dime store. She had shown

*Bennie Bedwell at a press conference, seated next to his attorney.*

Delores one photo of the man, leaning against a car, and another one from the waist up. According to Delores, Barbara mentioned him from time to time, saying that they had occasional dates and that she was crazy about him. Delores said she had not come forward sooner because she was afraid.

Both Mrs. Grimes and Bedwell's attorney disputed Delores' story. By this time, Loretta Grimes was intent on preserving the good memory and reputation of her daughters. Even if presented with hard evidence of promiscuity, she would have understandably refused to see it. Her statement was simple: "Barbara did not date," she said, "except with a couple of neighborhood boys who would come over."

David Bradshaw also dismissed the claims of Bedwell being Barbara's boyfriend. He stated that Bedwell had been away from Chicago for much of the time that he was allegedly dating Barbara

- although he was forced to admit that he had been in the city in September 1955, and then was away again until April 1956.

And Bedwell would soon be leaving Chicago again - but not in the way he intended.

Since his release from jail, Bedwell had been working at a job that had been arranged for him by Bradshaw at the Salvation Army Men's Social Center at 509 North Union Avenue. He started each morning with breakfast at 6:30 a.m., after which he worked in the center's repair shop where he painted furniture until 4:00 p.m. In addition to room and board at the center, he received $1 per day for his labors. By keeping him working, and with a 10:00 p.m. curfew, Bedwell was kept away from his old life on West Madison Street. Bedwell seemed content with how things were going for him. "I've done learned my lesson," he told a reporter.

**Bennie Bedwell with his mother, shortly after it was learned that murder charges against him were about to be dismissed.**

On March 1, States Attorney Benjamin Adamowski announced that the murder charges against Bedwell would be dropped at a hearing on March 4. He stated that because of the certainty of the pathologist's findings that the girls had died on December 28, witnesses who saw Bedwell with the sisters after that date were well-meaning, but mistaken. He added that the sheriff's department had misled him into believing Bedwell's "seemingly absurd" confession. He refused to consider any further evidence that Lohman brought to him concerning Bedwell's guilt and even when Harry Glos promised a new witness who had first-hand knowledge of the sordid relationship between Bedwell and the sister, Adamowski ignored it.

Bedwell was now feeling good. He was celebrating his birthday with birthday cake and the good news that the charges against him were being dropped. Newspaper reporters caught up with him at his mother's home on West Monroe Street on March 3. He was enjoying the cake and pondering his future plans.

But Bedwell's new-found freedom lasted about as long as his birthday party did. Newspaper stories about the Grimes sisters' murders and Bedwell's arrest had circulated around the country, including to Volusia County, Florida. The county sheriff there, Hardie Daughtery, had been searching for Bedwell for a year in connection with the rape of a thirteen-year-old girl. She and a friend, age fourteen, had met Bedwell and another man at a carnival where he worked in Deland. They had invited the two men home and introduced them to her parents as "Bennie Bedwell" and "Indian John." The girls disappeared after attending a movie with the two men and were reported missing by their fathers the next day. Sheriff's deputies found them three days later in an abandoned trailer on the outskirts of town, where they had been left with some food and a dire warning from their captors that they were not to leave. They'd been beaten and raped and when the story of the Grimes sisters appeared in the local newspaper, the thirteen-year-old took the clippings to Sheriff Daughtery and identified her attacker as former carnival roustabout, Bennie Bedwell. Daughtery didn't follow through on the report, but watched the events in Chicago very closely. When he realized that Bedwell was not going to be charged with the Grimes sisters' murders, he contacted Sheriff Lohman in Cook County and set a warrant in motion.

Lohman must have gotten some grim satisfaction from handing Bedwell over to Florida authorities. Needless to say, he wanted to see the drifter prosecuted for the murders that he was convinced that he had committed but, by that point, he likely figured that a sentence for rape in Florida was better than no justice at all.

Lohman kept the arrangement with Sheriff Doughtery a closely-guarded secret, even refusing to offer details to reporters on the day that the arrest occurred. Lohman was at odds with all of the other law enforcement agencies in Chicago over the handling of the Grimes investigation. From the start, it had been a bungled mess and it grew worse as time went on. Things were so bad by early March 1957 that Lohman had asked for a special grand jury investigation into the conduct in the investigation, which State's Attorney Benjamin Adamowski called "unnecessary." The sheriff and the state's attorney were engaged in all-out battle over the case. Adamowski, when dismissing the charges against Bedwell, had told reporters that "it would be a folly to prolong this unfortunate episode."

Lohman, angry over the fact that Adamowski refused to even look at any of the additional evidence obtained by Harry Glos, fired back by sending a letter to Chief Justice Wilburt F. Crowley, asking for the grand jury investigation. He wanted someone to look into the actions of the state's attorney's office, coroner's office, police department, and even Lohman's own sheriff's department.

In the midst of all of this, State Senator Robert Graham of Chicago called for a legislative inquiry into both the Grimes and Schuessler-Peterson cases, charging that the police agencies involved were withholding information from each other and compromising the investigations -- a commonly-known fact to anyone involved with the case. Senator Arthur Bidwill of River Forest argued with Graham, saying that Chicago murders were none of the senate's business.

The whole beleaguered mess only proved that none of the authorities in the case trusted one another. They were so worried about defending their own part of the case that they had forgotten the big picture -- and had forgotten about the tragic victims.

What would have happened if the various departments actually had worked together? Would the case have been solved? We will never know, but one thing we can say for sure is that Barbara and Patricia Grimes, and their family, deserved better than what they were given.

On Monday, March 4, a laughing Bennie Bedwell exited the courthouse after hearing that the charges against him for the murder of Patricia and Barbara Grimes had been dismissed. As he was smiling for newspaper photographers, he was re-arrested on a fugitive warrant from Florida. As Bedwell was ushered into the Bedford Park police station, his attorney blustered outside and demanded to see his client. The officers ignored him and Bedwell was brought out twenty-five minutes later in handcuffs. He was taken back into the courthouse and the warrant was presented to the court. Since the rape statute in Florida carried a life sentence - or the death penalty - Bedwell should have been held without bail. Justice of the Peace Irving Eiserman set bail anyway at $100,000, which Bedwell could never pay. He was sent back to the County Jail with an extradition hearing that was set for March 25.

In the end, Bedwell did go back to Florida on the rape charges but, largely due to the amount of time that had passed, he managed to avoid a conviction. Was he guilty? Probably. Was he involved with the Grimes sisters' death? Again, he probably was, but how much, and to what extent?

No one knows and no one was ever able to prove it. Bedwell took the truth of this guilt and innocence to the grave.

# FADING INTO HISTORY

Harry Glos refused to let go of the case. Even after being dismissed and ignored by the state's attorney's office, he kept working on the investigation. On March 10, the witness that he had

*Investigator Harry Glos, who never gave up on the case. The Grimes' murders haunted him for the rest of his life.*

promised earlier, who asked that his identity not be revealed, became front page news in the *Chicago American*. The witness, a tree surgeon and U.S. Army veteran, was positive that he had seen the Grimes sisters with Bennie Bedwell in a tavern on West Madison Street on January 5. The man was afraid to report what he had seen and in fact, had waited until February 20 before coming forward. He only did so after the coroner's investigator had lost his job. He said, "I figured that if Mr. Glos could give up his job for what he thinks is right, I should come forward."

Earlier that evening, the witness and a friend

had gone to an auto show at an indoor arena called the International Amphitheater, which was located on the city's South Side at Halsted and 42nd Street. After leaving the arena, the two men drove north on Halsted Street and then turned left onto West Madison Street. As they drove through Skid Row, an area that was unknown to the two men, they decided to stop for a beer at one of the bars. They ordered and a few minutes later, two girls came in and walked straight to the women's restroom. The witness said that he mentioned to his friend that they looked awfully young to be in a bar. The two girls left the restroom and went outside, but one of the girls - the taller one who wore blue jeans - came back in and sat at the bar. She didn't drink anything and she soon left.

Shortly afterward, the witness and his friend left, too. They were drawn by the country music that was played at a bar across the street. They went over there and again saw the two girls. The band was playing and the girls were dancing together in their stocking feet, doing a kind of "jitterbug step." Again, the witness noted how young the girls looked.

He described a man who was sitting nearby with sideburns and long hair as Bennie Bedwell. "I never forget a face," he swore to the reporter. He had seen Bedwell clearly and he added that one of the girls had looked him straight in the eye several times. "That girl was Barbara," he said.

Harry Glos was also interviewed for the story. He said that he was convinced the witness was telling the truth and was not mistaken. He passed the information on to the state's attorney and asked that he be brought before a grand jury to tell his story. He further asked that the state's attorney share his original notes from the autopsies (not the pathology reports, but his own notes) and asked that the slides from the Chicago Police Laboratory be subpoenaed so that it could be proven that the girls were sexually active and that they had been violently attacked prior to death. Glos refused to back off with his efforts to see the truth exposed concerning the violence and sexual attacks on the girls. Without this evidence, he didn't believe the case would ever be solved. But it was not to be. Once again, Glos was ignored and dismissed, as he would continue to be in the years that followed.

Glos ran for election in the sheriff's race the following year, but lost. He managed to remain a frequent figure in the newspapers during the years that followed. He spoke to various groups in the city, was interviewed about juvenile crime, and spoke out to warn young people about this "new fad of hitchhiking." But he never forgot about Barbara and Patricia Grimes and he never gave up hoping that one day, their murders would be solved.

There were still a few attempts to investigate the case, but they were fewer and further between in the weeks that followed. In March, Gary Lindsay of Monroe City, Indiana, made calls to the Grimes home that resulted in his arrest. Lindsay had told Theresa Grimes over the telephone that her sisters' clothing was hidden under a trestle in the Chicago & Eastern Illinois Railroad yards in Dolton, Illinois. During one call, he told her that he was afraid of talking to her because her line was tapped. Theresa gave him the number of a nearby restaurant and he began calling her there. The police traced the call and took him in for questioning. Lindsay, a nineteen-year-old railroad switchman, was arrested carrying a fountain pen-type container with live tear gas cartridges for which he had no explanation. Not surprisingly, when the trestle was searched, the sisters' clothing was nowhere to be found.

The month of April brought no news to speak of and by summer, the newspaper stories and the speculation had basically come to an end. There was barely a notice when news came in August that Bennie Bedwell had been found not guilty of statutory rape in Florida.

In October, the case was mentioned again in the papers when Mrs. Grimes received a postage due envelope in the mail that contained a rosary and a single white bobby sock. Hope surfaced once again when Loretta said that the sock was the same type the girls were wearing on the night they disappeared. Jimmy Grimes said that Patricia often borrowed his rosary, which was just like the one that came in the mail. Sadly, though, the family was grasping at straws. They had lost all faith in the authorities by this time and even the slightest hint of a clue filled them with hope. The envelope also contained a piece of paper with a message on one side, written in blue crayon: "Me see police not get some place remember woman hear girl scream." The other side had another (just as nonsensical) message: "Me find this in alley Jan 20 boy clean car like crazy 3528

Damen." The family rushed to the address that was listed - it was an empty lot.

On April 1959, a newspaper story appeared with a heading that read "Memories of Bizarre Case are Revived." The story was about how a simple marriage ceremony had renewed interest in the unsolved murders of the Grimes sisters. Theresa Grimes had married Angelo Campanale, a thirty-year-old furniture salesman, and a ceremony that had been attended by one hundred friends and relatives. Joseph Grimes had given away the bride and Theresa's married sister, Shirley Wojcik, served as one of the attendants. Loretta Grimes, the newsman noted, was solemn and dry-eyed and watched from a pew with her sons, Joseph and James.

On August 12, 1960, Bennie Bedwell was back in the news while he was being sought on a petty larceny charge. Sangamon County Sheriff Hugh Campbell, from Springfield, Illinois, said a warrant had been issued for Bedwell after a complaint from his employer, a junk dealer named Casper Sullivan. Bedwell had come to Springfield in the spring of 1960 while working for a traveling carnival. He stayed in town after obtaining work with the junk dealer. The two became friends and Bedwell often stayed late at the Sullivan home, drinking with the junkman and his wife, Virginia.

The police were contacted by Sullivan after Bedwell failed to show up for work on July 22, the same day that Sullivan discovered that $22 was missing from a money sack at the junkyard. But who had taken it? Apparently, Sullivan's wife, Virginia, had disappeared just hours before Bedwell was last seen. She was last spotted carrying two suitcases and getting into a car driven by another woman.

The Grimes sisters' case was back in the news again in September 1961. Texas authorities had arrested a thirty-two-year-old man named John Edwin Myers for his part in an Illinois to Texas weekend murder spree that resulted in the deaths of four people. On September 18, Myers was indicted for the murder of Arthur Lee Dekraai, an Ottumwa, Iowa, hitchhiker that he killed near Big Spring, Texas. Dekraai had been picked up in a stolen car, driven by Myers, during the crime spree. He killed the hitchhiker for his money -- the grand sum of $16.

But Myers did not take part in this crime spree alone. His accomplice was Donna Stone, his thirteen-year-old mistress, who admitted taking part in the four murders. She was wanted by Missouri authorities for the murder of Margaret Wernicker, a St. Louis department store worker, who was killed near Thayer, Missouri. The pair had also admitted killing George Ballard and his daughter, Carol, age ten, near their Belleville, Illinois, home.

In March 1962, Myers was sentenced to death for Dekraai's murder. The jury in the case deliberated for only two hours after Dr. James Krelmeyer, from Texas' State Hospital for the Insane, testified that Myers was not psychotic and knew the difference between right and wrong.

Donna Stone was extradited to Illinois when she turned fourteen, because she could be tried as an adult for murder. She expressed no emotion as she pled guilty to reduced manslaughter charges for the killings of George and Carol Ballard. Stone had been visiting her grandparents in Edwardsville, Illinois, when she met Myers the previous summer. They lived together in Chicago but returned to Edwardsville together in August 1961. To get a car to leave the area, Myers and Stone held up the Ballards, who had been fishing at a local lake. Stone tied the victims' hands with clothesline and Myers shot them in the head. Then, unable to get the car started, the pair walked to a nearby home, stole a car, and kidnapped Margaret Wernicker. The next day, near Thayer, Missouri, they took Margaret into a lonely field where, Stone confessed, she shot the woman twice in the back. She then took Margaret's clothes and shoes, which she was wearing when she was arrested.

Circuit Clerk Richard T. Carter placed her in the custody of the Illinois Youth Commission, where she was held at the State Training School for Girls in Geneva until she was twenty-one. She later appeared before the parole and pardon board, was imprisoned for seven more years, and then was released after fourteen years behind bars.

But how did this connect to the Grimes sisters?

The Chicago police became interested in the case after the pair's arrest. Myers, who had worked as a dishwasher in Chicago, had shared an apartment at 2622 West 38th Street with Stone at the time of several unsolved murders in the region, including the murders of the Grimes sisters. Detective Howard Felker was sent to Texas to question Myers, but he was unable to link the killers to the Grimes murders.

At the height of the Grimes case, there were scores of mental patients, eccentrics, and cranks who confessed to the murders of the two young women. In addition to Bennie Bedwell and his multiple confessions, there was a transient who claimed to have been involved in the crime, only to have his story unravel.

One alleged confession -- about which little documentation exists -- came from a seventeen-year-old named Max Fleig. He was picked up by a suspect, but the current law did not allow juveniles to be given a polygraph test. However, Captain Ralph Petaque persuaded the boy to take the test anyway and in the middle of it, he claimed that Fleig confessed to kidnapping the sisters and killing them. The story went on to say that because the test was illegal and inadmissible, the police were forced to let Fleig go free. Was he the killer? No one will ever know -- or if this story is actually true. It is said that Fleig ended up being sent to prison a few years later for the brutal murder of a young woman.

But perhaps the most sensational confession in the aftermath of the murders came from California on December 28, 1962, the sixth anniversary of the date when the Grimes sisters disappeared. It was on that day that a prisoner, about to be released from serving sixty days on a drunkenness charge, confessed to the murders. The prisoner, Alfred Smith Lawless, told police and newsmen: "Six years ago today I killed Barbara and Patricia Grimes and I've been running ever since. I see visions of those two girls all the time. All I think about lately is how I left them to die, stripped and naked on that snowbank in the woods. For years I've been running. I just had to tell somebody."

Lawless, a thirty-four-year-old machine operator and drifter, who said that he was from Jamestown, Kentucky, told police that he had picked up the girls at a Chicago theater where an Elvis Presley movie was playing, molested them, choked and bound them, then threw them from an automobile. Lawless' account was eerily similar to that of Bennie Bedwell, but included other details, like an excellent description of the girls, the clothing they wore on the night of the disappearance, and knowledge of Patricia's crooked toe. All of these things -- even the toe -- had appeared in newspaper articles about the case, although the toe had not been widely reported.

Lawless was quoted as saying, "I had to tell somebody about the murders. I'm scared that if I didn't do it, I might do the same thing again to other innocent girls."

He told reporters that he met the girls when they left the theater. He continued with his account: "I struck up a casual conversation with them. They agreed to go with me to my car to get hamburgers. I had never seen them before. We drove out to the country. Then I stopped the car and made love to them. I got scared, figured they might tell somebody about it. I had been drinking. It's fuzzy about how exactly I did it, but I remember taking off their clothes and leaving them in the snow bank.

"It seems like I knocked them unconscious somehow. I burned all their clothes, their slacks, blouses, coats and got rid of their shoes and purses. Then I got out of town.

"I went to Indiana, then Detroit. I've been all over the country running ever since."

In addition to the Grimes sisters, Lawless also claimed that he had murdered a man named Walter "Pea-John" Miller in Jamestown, Kentucky, in "1947 or 1948." Los Angeles Police Lieutenant John A. Tidyman quoted Lawless as saying that he hit Miller on the head, robbed him, and ran over him with a car to make it look like a traffic accident. Miller's body had been found in Southeast Kentucky, near Jamestown, and no arrest had ever been made. However, Kentucky Judge T.A. Miller said that Miller died in 1953 or 1954, not at the time claimed by Lawless, but that the details he provided in that case warranted a closer look. Kentucky officials were curious enough to send Sheriff Bob McClendon to Los Angeles to bring Lawless back to Jamestown.

But the cops in Chicago were not as curious. Even the Los Angeles detectives were skeptical of Lawless' story. "We want to make sure that he's a good suspect, and not some guy looking for a free ride back to Chicago," one of the detectives told the newsmen.

Chicago police and sheriff's officers had no immediate plans to fly to Los Angeles to question Lawless. Chicago homicide detective John Keane told reporters: "We don't discount -- we hope it's the real thing -- but we have to learn more about it."

Lieutenant Walter A. Weingart of the Cook County Sheriff's Department said: "There are discrepancies in his story, but of course we will check it out. Frankly, I'm a little dubious."

And detectives had every right to be. As Los Angeles investigators began checking into Lawless' story, it slowly came apart. Initially, they were suspect of his account because autopsy reports had shown that the Grimes sisters had not been sexually molested or violently treated. They had simply frozen to death. How they ended up on the roadway was unknown. Of course, in time, it would be revealed that the initial autopsy findings were flawed, but it was not Lawless who had violated those young women.

It was Lawless' background that finally destroyed his story. The Kentucky drifter had served time in the military during World War II and had been discharged in 1947 -- into a mental institution. Alfred Smith Lawless' chilling account of how he raped and murdered Barbara and Patricia Grimes was nothing more than the product of a damaged mind.

# WHO KILLED THE GRIMES SISTERS?

Over time, the Grimes case disappeared from the newspapers, but it took many years for it to fade from Chicago's collective memory. But eventually, it did fade away. For the most part, the only people who remembered the story were aging friends, the last few family members, and the neighbors in McKinley Park, who hung onto their homes and churches through changing times and eras. Occasionally, on some anniversary, the story appeared in the

**Police officers looking down the slope from German Church Road where the bodies of the Grimes sisters were found.**

newspapers again, usually as one of the city's great unsolved crimes. Every once in a while, the girls would rate a mention in a book about true crime or unsolved murders, but for the most part, those who didn't live in Chicago had never heard of the two lost girls.

But it never faded from the minds of the veteran detectives and graying principals of the case, all of whom were haunted by the fact that Barbara and Patricia's killer was never found.

There were countless theories that swirled about concerning the deaths of the two girls. In many cases, we can blame the era on the fact that a crime went unsolved. We can say that the forensic methods of the day were not what they are today, or there was too much confusion and lack of cooperation between the police jurisdictions. And while those things did play a part in the failure to solve the Grimes case, they were not the sole reason why the killer got away. This was a case that would have even greatly challenged modern police departments. Every part of the case presented challenges and multiple mysteries, from the myriad of contradictory sightings and eyewitness accounts to the time of death and the placement of the bodies on German Church Road. As we reach any sort of conclusion in the case, another issue comes along that makes it implausible.

No theory ever presented can explain where the girls were killed or when, which brings up the question of how they could have been there on the side of the road without being seen. If they were killed and dumped on December 28, how did no one see them? If they were placed there just before they were found, how do we explain the melting and thawing of ice and the weather conditions?

The list of reasons why the case was never solved continued to grow over the years (and continues today) with revelations about autopsy reports, sexual abuse, rumors, and innuendoes about the two sisters and what kinds of behavior that they may -- or may not -- have been involved in.

Many of the theories that have been presented over the years are just plain ridiculous, often involving people like the alleged psychic Walter Kranz or Leonard Prescott, the man who first discovered the bodies on German Church Road on that cold January day.

Others are more compelling, or at least simply refuse to go away. A couple of years ago, I was contacted by two former police officers, who believed that they had a solution to the case. They were sure that the girls had been kidnapped by some teenage boys that were acquainted with Theresa Grimes. What had happened to the girls after that, no one knew, but they were sure that these boys were involved. Because some of these boys are still alive, I won't print any of their names in this book, mostly because there's no actual proof that they were involved, but it was a compelling theory.

Other theories about the case date all the way back to 1956, while others are simply enduring beliefs that remain with investigators who still ponder the case today. Officially, the murders of the Grimes sisters remain open and unsolved. The girls have not been forgotten, but whether or not their killer will ever be found remains open for debate.

Here are a few of the most intriguing theories that have been suggested about the murders, as well as my own thoughts on the heartbreaking case.

### Charles Leroy Melquist

The links between Charles Melquist and the Grimes sisters case are downright chilling and it's possible -- perhaps event likely -- that he had something to do with the murders. We do know that he was convicted of a similar murder and even as far back as 1958, police detectives believed that he might have murdered Barbara and Patricia, as well.

On September 22, Bonnie Leigh Scott vanished. That evening, around 6:30 p.m., she left the home where she lived in Addison, Illinois, and told her grandmother that she was going out to look for a blouse. Bonnie lived with her aunt and uncle, Mrs. Robert Schwolow; their daughter, Sue, age fifteen; and Bonnie's maternal grandmother, Mrs. Doris Hitchins. Her parents were separated and in the midst of a divorce. Bonnie was an ordinary girl, a sophomore at York Community High School and a babysitter for many of the young children who lived in the quiet suburban community. The five-room, newly built ranch house where she lived was virtually identical to all of the others on the street. Before the night of September 22, Bonnie never caused a problem, never drew much attention, and seemed like every other girl her age. But that night, she became a mystery.

As the police began tracing her steps, assuming that she was a runaway, they managed to find four teenagers who saw her at a diner in Addison around 7:30 p.m. that night. She was also seen at a surplus store, located next door to the town's police station.

After that, she had apparently vanished into thin air.

It turned out that Bonnie was not exactly the ordinary high school girl that everyone assumed she was. She had lived in Addison for three years at the time of her disappearance. Her parents had separated and her father had packed up and moved out west, abandoning Bonnie, and his wife, Marilyn. That was when Bonnie was sent to live with her uncle, aunt, and grandmother. At one point, when she was an eighth grader, she told a friend that she wanted to run away and visit her father out west. The friend, who later spoke to newspaper reporters anonymously, talked her out of it.

The police initially assumed Bonnie was a runaway because she had done it before. One weekend she disappeared with another of her friends and spent the weekend in the city. She also occasionally skipped school. Once, after she was caught in the company of another truant, her friend told her that they had better "knuckle down and take their schooling seriously so they wouldn't end up like the Grimes sisters."

On September 23, a man named Charles Melquist telephoned Bonnie's home. The twenty-three-year-old stone worker from Villa Park told Jean Schwolow that he had received two telephone calls concerning a man with whom Bonnie Leigh had quarreled. Jean called the police and reported the information.

Melquist, repeating his story for William Devaney, an Addison police detective, said that Bonnie had called him at 8:15 on the evening of her disappearance and said that she had misgivings about the man she was with. She hung up on him abruptly after Melquist told her that it was her own problem. Melquist told police that he and Bonnie were friends and that she often consulted him as a sort of "big brother," and that he regretted not being more patient with her call.

He also told Detective Devaney about the second telephone call, which came that night around 11:00 p.m. from a young man that he didn't know. The caller said that Bonnie had gotten out of his car near Mannheim Road and U.S. Route 66 after an argument and wanted Melquist to bring her home. Melquist said that he went to the spot, but found no trace of the girl.

Police detectives continued the search for the girl, but what few clues they had led nowhere. They searched for the young man that Bonnie was allegedly out with that night, trying to trace the names that were in a small white address book found in Bonnie's room. They questioned thirty-eight young men (two of them were later given lie detector tests) but the trail soon petered out and went cold.

Then, on November 15, 1958, a group of Boy Scouts on a nature hike in the Argonne Woods forest preserve made a gruesome discovery in a gulley off of La Grange Road -- the nude, decapitated body of a young girl. The dump site was just a few miles from where the nude, frozen bodies of the Grimes sisters had been discovered less than two years before.

Police were called to the scene and the horrific discovery soon made the newspapers. On Sunday morning, about 9:00 a.m., Addison detectives received a call from Doris Hitchins, Bonnie's grandmother. "I wonder if that could be my granddaughter?" she asked.

After contacting, Nels Anderson, the acting Addison police chief, detectives called the Chicago morgue for a general description of the body. The corpse's hair had been tinted red, the same as Bonnie's was. The fingernails were coated with the same silver nail polish used by the missing girl. A wristwatch was found about twenty feet from the decapitated body, near the head, that was the same type as the one that Bonnie wore. The Addison detectives were reasonably sure that they had found the missing girl.

At this point, the small suburban department contacted the Chicago police, who sent a squad to assist. Among them were two crime scene technicians, who fingerprinted everything in Bonnie's house that might have her prints on it. They also collected a bottle of silver nail polish from her bedroom. Addison detectives contacted Bonnie's dentist, Dr. P.D. Grimes of Elmhurst, and took him to the Chicago city morgue to examine the skull. With a full set of her dental x-rays in hand, he looked closely at the skull's upper teeth and announced that he was "very assured" that the body found in the woods was that of Bonnie Leigh Scott. He told detectives, "There's too much similarity, I'm quite sure it's her."

Chicago Police Lieutenant James McMahon later stated that the girl appeared to have been killed with a large knife. He said that two gashes had been cut into her abdomen and it looked as though a large knife had been used to sever her head. He told newspaper reporters on Monday, November 17, that a number of leads were being pursued, including a search of a pond near the spot where the body was found in hopes of finding the girl's missing clothes.

The newspapers were quick to draw comparisons between Bonnie's case and that of the Grimes sisters. The sisters had also been missing for several weeks before their nude bodies were found on the side of a wooded road, just a few miles from where Bonnie was found.

And the newspapers were not the only ones to make the connection.

On the night of November 16, the day after Bonnie's body was discovered, the telephone rang at the home of Loretta Grimes, mother of Barbara and Patricia. Strange, late-night, anonymous calls were nothing new for members of the Grimes family. They had been subjected to numerous incidents of heavy breathing, cruel pranks, and menacing laughter. But this call was different.

This time, the caller said to Mrs. Grimes: "I've committed another perfect crime. This is another one those cops won't solve and they're not going to hook it onto Bedwell or Barry Cook."

He laughed after making this reference to Edward "Bennie" Bedwell, who confessed and then was released in the murder case of her daughters, and Barry Cook, who admitted and then denied his involvement in two 1957 murders. By then, he was serving time at Joliet Penitentiary for other crimes.

Loretta said that the man hung up after that, but not before she recognized his voice. She was later quoted as saying, "I will never forget that voice."

She was positive that the man had called her in May 1957, claimed that he knew who had killed the girls, and that he had helped undress them. Loretta did not hear from the man again until after Bonnie's body was found, but she certainly remembered what he said to her: "I know something about your little girl that no one else knows but you -- not even the police. The smallest girl's toes were crossed on both of her feet." After revealing this little-known deformity, the man laughed cruelly and then hung up.

The identity of the caller was never uncovered, but could it have been another man who liked to call suffering relatives with strange telephone calls? A man like Charles Melquist, who had called Bonnie Scott's aunt after her disappearance with tantalizing clues that hampered the police investigation? There are some who theorize that Melquist committed both crimes. They even believe that, after it was revealed that Melquist smothered Bonnie Leigh, that this might explain why officials had such a hard time pinning down the cause of death for the Grimes sisters. Could they have been smothered too?

Melquist was certainly on the top of the list of people that detectives wanted to question after Bonnie's body was found. The information that he had provided to detectives about the two telephone calls that he had received on the night she was last seen had always seemed suspicious, but they had no reason to interrogate him -- until now.

Detectives spent Sunday afternoon, November 16, trying to track down his whereabouts. When he heard that the police were looking for him, he walked into the station voluntarily around 11:30 p.m. to answer questions. Melquist sat down with William Devaney, as well as Chicago detectives, and he was asked to tell the story of the two phone calls that he had received on the night of Bonnie's disappearance. They also asked him about his relationship with the victim. Devaney later said, "At the time, his story didn't seem too good. Each time we asked him to repeat something for some reason, he would go back and start his story all over again."

The investigators decided to let Melquist leave, with strict instructions that he return to the station the next morning. At this point, they left him with the feeling that he was helping out with the case, not that he was a suspect. Chief Anderson drove him home around 2:30 a.m., and during the drive, he talked to the chief about how he wanted to join the police someday.

Meanwhile, the police were busy impounding Melquist's 1958 silver Chevrolet, which had been left at the station. It later turned out to be the car that he killed Bonnie in.

On Monday morning at 10:00 a.m., Melquist returned to the police station. He told the same story over again and detectives were now convinced that he had memorized it. Chicago detectives offered to send for a polygraph machine and it arrived at the station later that day. After two juveniles were hooked up to the machine (they were among the three dozen or so young men whose names were found in Bonnie's address book) and were dismissed from further interrogation, Melquist was given the first of two lie detector tests at the station.

Devaney later said, "He failed rather miserably, giving what seemed to be definitely a correct answer only once in twenty chances. He was taken into another room and told to relax for a while with the thought that he may have been too tense during the first test. He flunked in practically the same manner on the second test, however, and then seemed to get a little excited."

The detectives agreed that Melquist would be taken for another examination, this time by John Reid, a famed master interrogator and polygraph expert. Reid ran a private firm, John E. Reid & Associates at 600 South Michigan Avenue, where police officers often took major suspects who refused to confess. Reid was a native Chicagoan, who joined the police force in 1939, the same year that he took the bar exam and was admitted to the Illinois bar. He worked as a beat cop for a time and then was the first policeman assigned to the Chicago Crime Laboratory after it was taken over from Northwestern University. From 1942 to 1947, he was in charge of administering lie detector tests for the department. In 1947, he resigned and started a private firm. Reid and his associates were responsible for clearing a number of Chicago murder cases and also for ruling out scores of men who had been suspected in heinous crimes. For the department of the late 1950s, there was no one better at getting the guilty to confess -- and freeing the innocent -- than John Reid. He would soon uphold that reputation with Charles Melquist.

The detectives left Addison with Melquist at 2:00 p.m., planning to deliver him to Reid's office that afternoon. Detective Devaney later recounted that they stopped for a meal at a local restaurant and he said that Melquist made a comment that seemed to indicate that he knew the "jig was up." He added, "The condemned man ate a hearty meal."

At 4:00 p.m., Melquist was taken to Reid's office and the third polygraph test was administered. After that, things moved quickly and by 6:45, he had signed a preliminary confession to Bonnie's murder that was six or seven pages long. He was then taken to the offices of the Cook County State's Attorney, and from there, contact was made with the DuPage Sheriff, Stanley Lynch, since the crime had actually taken place in Villa Park. By 10:00 p.m. that night,

Melquist had been handed over to the DuPage County Sheriff's Department and officially booked for the murder of Bonnie Leigh Scott.

As word reached the newspapers that Melquist had confessed to the murder, neighbors began to speak out about the man -- and disturbing information came to light about Melquist's contact with Bonnie and scores of other young girls, whose names and telephone numbers were later found in his possession.

Police officers stood guard at Melquist's home at 655 South Yale Avenue in Villa Park. They refused to allow access to reporters to the home, but neighbors and acquaintances of the young man painted a stark picture of a person they barely knew, even though he had lived next door to them for more than fifteen years.

Melquist, a slender, dark-haired man of average height, wore a thin mustache to hide the scar of a hair lip operation and was described by one person who knew him, a short order cook at an Addison diner, as a "ladies man." The cook told reporters, "He had a little black book with the names of girls in most of the western suburbs. He didn't have many boy friends. He drove his car like a madman and he'd drive all over the county just to see a good western or a war movie. He was crazy about them, especially double and triple features if they were all about the same thing."

In the Villa Park neighborhood where Melquist lived, female neighbors were chilled by the revelations about the man, but were not particularly surprised. Two young women said that he was "egotistical" and a loner, who didn't mingle with other students when he attended York Community High School in Elmhurst. He was always worried about looking "slick" to his female friends. During the two years he was in high school, from 1952 to 1954, he became a "behavior problem" at the school. Nothing terrible stood out, according to William Mueller, the boy's dean, but he "became known to the dean's office." Melquist was a below average student, who was very unhappy when things didn't go his way.

Neighbors on South Yale Avenue, noted that he was "overly quiet." Mrs. Amanda Nelson called him "mischievous, but not bad, you know, just given to pranks" when Melquist was a boy. One of the women who lived nearby on the shadowy, tree-lined, and poorly lit street, shuddered when she pointed out Melquist's home to a reporter.

While Melquist was writing confessions, the police were busy building a case against him, interviewing witnesses and collecting information. In a statement to reporters, Chief Anderson promised that Melquist was being linked even closer to Bonnie, who he claimed had been a girlfriend who originally told him that she was seventeen. According to two girls that knew Bonnie, she had told them that she planned to see Melquist on the night she was killed. In addition, two teenage boys also reported that Melquist became excited and ran from a bowling alley when news came that Bonnie's body had been found in the forest preserve.

Soon, others began coming forward with more information, including that he might also have a background in burglary. A Texas woman named Hope McCarver, age nineteen, who claimed to be Melquist's girlfriend, told police that the unemployed stone mason once confided to her that he was "supposed to go out on a burglary job at a factory with two or three buddies."

McCarver, who hoped to marry Melquist after divorcing her first husband, said that the young man made the statement during a "tryst" at his Villa Park home. She said that she didn't know if he had gone through with the plans.

Meanwhile, another young woman, Arlene Rullo, told police that Melquist tried to choke her while she sat in a parked car with him. She had gone out with him in November 1957, before she was married. She said that Melquist stopped his car and tried to kiss her, but she refused. He then bragged about the "judo holds" that he learned in the Army and put his hands around her neck. Rullo told the police: "When I came to, he was sitting beside me, staring at me with a strange look in his eyes. He said, 'Gee, I didn't realize what I was doing. Believe me, I'm real sorry.'"

Two other young woman also came forward to allege that Melquist had also tried to choke them while on dates. Both attacks had taken place within the last eighteen months.

But nothing that the police learned was as chilling as the words that came directly from the mouth of Charles Melquist. On Tuesday, the lanky young man re-enacted the gruesome crime.

The journey began in the driveway of Melquist's home in Villa Park, where he stood staring at where his car had been parked on September 22. "I killed her there," he mumbled, reiterating what he had told police in his two written confessions. The second confession had been forty-five pages long. He added, "I'm sorry about it all. I don't care what happens to me."

Melquist had led the police officers into his home, where he pointed out two pink, satin-colored pillows. With one of them -- he could not recall which one -- he had smothered Bonnie while they were sitting in his car. He told police that Bonnie had asked him to meet her that night and they stopped at his home for a short time. When they returned to the car, she was "goofing around, then we started wrestling around. I grabbed a pillow and must have held it too long." When he was asked what he meant by that, Melquist replied, "Because the next thing I knew, she didn't move anymore."

He had then taken off her clothing, stuffed it under the car seat, and set out to find a place where her body could be hidden where there was little chance it would be found.

Melquist was then taken by Cook County and DuPage County authorities south and east along the route that he followed to LaGrange Road, about a mile south of 95th Street, where he dumped her body in a gulley where the Argonne forest preserve bordered the highway. He told detectives, "I pushed it across the guard rail just like a sack. She was lying on her back. I dragged her by the feet down the embankment fifteen feet to this small thicket. Then I left."

Melquist, who told police officers that he believed he had dreamed of the murder, told investigators that he returned to the site. He told Tom Cook, a Cook County deputy sheriff, "I came back the following Friday just to make sure she was there. I came back about three weeks ago. I had a knife and pitchfork in my car. I was going to dig a grave."

With the knife, Melquist admitted that he had cut off Bonnie's head and kicked it several feet away, and then he made several deep gashes in her body. He told investigators that he had "an urge to cut."

He said that he had horrible dreams after mutilating Bonnie's body. He kept dreaming, he said, of cutting people up into pieces.

As the long caravan of cars containing police officers, prosecuting attorneys, reporters, and cameramen traveled north on LaGrange Road, heading back to Villa Park, Melquist pointed out a section of roadside where he had disposed of the knife. A search was ordered of the area, but Melquist claimed to be unsure of where

114

he had thrown the knife, waving an arm along a half-mile of woods and roadside. Melquist said that he had burned Bonnie's clothing near Irving Park and Elmhurst Roads, but because he had been drinking at the time, he was unable to remember where he had done it. But he did recall that he was driving Bonnie's grandmother's car at the time. He had told Mrs. Hitchins that he was searching for the missing girl, but was destroying evidence instead.

Throughout the re-enactment, Melquist was handcuffed to Captain John Rode of the Cook County Sheriff's Police and accompanied by William J. Bauer, DuPage County First Assistant State's Attorney, Chief Deputy Smith, and Herbert Mertes and Stanley Lange, investigators for the DuPage County Sheriff. As the car ride continued, Melquist told them that he "hoped he got the chair," expressing a wish for the death sentence.

But Melquist was not going to get that wish if attorney Robert J. McDonnell got his way. While Melquist was being taken from the Bedford Park sheriff police station, where he had spent the night after his second confession, McDonnell was going into Criminal Court with Elmer Melquist, the young killer's father, and a psychiatrist, Dr. A.D. Hershfield. He told the court that both he and Melquist's father had been unable to talk to Melquist. He sought a writ of habeas corpus that would require formal charges to be filed against the young man and enable McDonnell to see his client. But the matter became pointless, however, when he learned that the confessed killer was already on his way to DuPage County and that Melquist was served with a murder warrant when he got there.

After the re-enactment, Melquist signed the forty-five page confession at the Villa Park jail. He was then taken to the DuPage County Jail in Wheaton. Melquist's father and attorney showed up a short time later and after a hurried conference with the confused, McDonnell said that the elder Melquist had "unswerving faith" in his son and did not believe any confession he might have made. "We are repudiating the confession on the basis of points I will make later in court," McDonnell told reporters. In addition, he refused any plans that Cook County and Chicago police officers had to subject Melquist to lie detector tests in several recent unsolved slayings -- especially those of the Grimes sisters. McDonnell said that he would not permit Melquist to take any more lie detector tests.

As too often happens in cases in which confessed killers end up with wily lawyers, Melquist immediately denied his two signed confessions. He had been "hypnotized" into confessing, he claimed. He had not killed Bonnie Leigh. The police, specifically polygraph operator John Reid, had tricked him into saying that he had.

This story continued at Melquist's April-May 1959 trial. The defense rested its case after Melquist took the stand and testified to being under a hypnotic spell during the confessions. The defense claimed that Reid "had some kind of pencil or something" and waved it back and forth while asking Melquist questions. He testified, "I was so tired I was ready to go back to sleep. It was some kind of feeling. I don't know what I would call it. It was almost like maybe you're hypnotized." He said that he was in that hypnotic trance when he confessed to Reid and was still under the effects of the same trance when he gave a much longer statement a short time later.

The jury was not impressed with his story. On May 2, they found him guilty of Bonnie's murder and on June 12, Melquist was formally sentenced to ninety-nine years in prison. Judge Mel Abrahamson of DuPage County Circuit Court imposed the sentenced after denying a motion for a new trial for Melquist. The former construction worker gulped nervously several times as Judge Abrahamson ordered him incarcerated at Joliet Penitentiary. When asked if he had anything to say for himself, he whispered, "No."

But his attorney, Robert McDonnell, had plenty to say. He immediately filed an appeal on Melquist's behalf, stating that his confession should have never been accepted as evidence. The courts didn't agree and the appeals were denied, but in the end, it didn't matter much. Of his ninety-nine year sentence, Melquist only served just over eleven years. He was paroled and later got married and had two children. He died in 2010, fifty years later than he deserved for the heinous crime for which he was convicted.

Melquist was convicted of Bonnie's murder, but did he get away with other murders that he was never even questioned about -- including those of Barbara and Patricia Grimes? There are those who believe that he did and that Charles Leroy Melquist was literally the man who got away with murder in the Grimes case.

As far back as 1958, Melquist was being linked to the Grimes murders. There is no question that there were some eerie similarities in the cases and some disturbing connections between Melquist and the Grimes case. Coincidences? Perhaps, but these links cause many to believe that Melquist was also the Grimes killer.

In addition to the basic facts in the case -- young girls gone missing, found stripped naked, possibly smothered to death, dumped in a wooded area on Chicago's Southwest Side -- the police also discovered some fairly direct links.

Two girls, whose names and former telephone numbers were discovered in Melquist's room in his Villa Park home, were neighbors of the Grimes sisters at the time the sisters disappeared in December 1956. However, the two girls told investigators that they did not know Melquist and had only a vague idea how he could have gotten their names and telephone numbers. Both told of strange calls to their homes about the time that Barbara and Patricia disappeared. The calls were made by a man who said he found their names and numbers on the back of bus seats.

The two girls, Sharon Blomberg and Diane Prunty, both fifteen-years-old, both lived near the Grimes sisters in the McKinley Park neighborhood. Sharon had formerly lived only two blocks from the girls and Diane was a half-mile away, straight across McKinley Park. They told investigators that they once frequented a candy shop at 35th Street and Archer Avenue that was also patronized by the Grimes sisters. They swam in McKinley Park and frequently went to the Brighton Theater, where the Grimes sisters were last seen. However, neither of the girls knew Barbara and Patricia personally. The Grimes sisters had attended parochial schools and Sharon and Diane both attended public school.

But the girls were only two of the young women on Melquist's list, which did not include the Grimes sisters. The police found a book filled with the names of seventy young women from the area, most of them teenagers. Detectives found that six of the women in Melquist's book told of being choked by him, sometimes into unconsciousness, while on dates. Melquist's knowledge of "judo," the police believed, allowed him to render a victim unconscious without leaving any signs of violence.

And this, some theorists believe, is what Melquist also did the Grimes sisters. They refuse to ignore the similarities between Bonnie's murder and the murders of Barbara and Patricia.

Like Bonnie, the Grimes sisters were found naked and their clothing was never found. Bonnie's body was too decomposed when it was found for pathologists to determine a cause of death. In the Grimes case, because no cause of death could be found, the autopsy reports were altered to say that they froze to death. According to Melquist, Bonnie had been smothered. It's been suggested that this could have happened to the Grimes sisters, too. The site where Bonnie's body was found is in the same general area on the Southwest Side as the place where Barbara and Patricia were found. Not far from both sites is Santa Fe Park, which was searched thoroughly for clues in the Grimes case. Melquist told investigators that he frequently went to the races in that park.

Was Charles Leroy Melquist, convicted killer of Bonnie Scott, also the man who killed the Grimes sisters? Some historians believe that he was and, no matter what the reader believes, there are a number of similarities between the cases.

But in the interest of honesty, this author believes they are nothing but that -- similarities. I personally believe (and this is only my opinion) that Melquist did not kill the Grimes sisters. Although I do believe that he was a sexual predator who took out his aggressions on teenage girls. I also think that he got a sexual charge out of stalking women with telephone calls. He collected his list of seventy young women, and while news reports focused on the two girls who lived near the Grimes sisters, because that was the more sensational story, I imagine that there were many more women on the list who received creepy calls from him. I also think that he was the one who called Loretta Grimes after the body of Bonnie Scott had been found in the woods. Her tearful reaction was just the sort of thing that Melquist wanted. The Grimes story was still big news in the area and Melquist, like the newspapers and many people who lived in the area, used the similarities in the case to hurt Mrs. Grimes.

After Bonnie went missing, Melquist couldn't help himself. He called the police and introduced the "mystery man" into the situation. He also wormed his way in with Bonnie's family, posing as her "big brother advisor" so that he could be part of the search. If he told anyone that he was her boyfriend, he might have looked guilty. This way, he seemed to be a helpful friend.

It is documented that Melquist "choked out" at least six of the women that he took out on dates. I imagine there were more who never came forward. In Bonnie's case, I believe that he took things too far and she actually died. I'm not even convinced that he meant to kill her. When he realized that he had, he went into a panic, took her clothes, and dumped her body -- just like someone had done with the Grimes sisters. Melquist was well aware of the facts in the Grimes case, and I believe that he purposely imitated the situation, perhaps thinking that this would draw attention away from him.

When Melquist returned to the scene of the body dump, he told police that he came to bury Bonnie. I don't believe this. I believe that he came back to the site to take satisfaction in what he had done. Like a depraved child, he decided to mutilate her body and cut off her head. He told the police that he dreamed about it, but a better way to describe it would be to say that he fantasized about cutting her up. Melquist had escalated from choking girls to killing them -- who knows what he might have done if he had never been caught?

Melquist was a coward, though. He stalked women with anonymous telephone calls, he choked them into unconsciousness so that he could have sex with them, and when the police caught up with him, he fell apart. Investigators weren't fooled by his obviously rehearsed story and before long, he had confessed to everything. Even though he later repudiated the confession, it was the truth, or at least as close to the truth as Melquist could manage. But if he confessed to killing Bonnie, then why not confess to killing the Grimes sisters, too? He couldn't confess to those murders because the only facts that he knew about the case were what had been printed in the newspaper. He didn't know the real details, the facts that the police had held back to weed out the nuts and cranks who always turned out to confess, because he had nothing to do with their deaths.

I admit that Charles Melquist makes an attractive candidate for Barbara and Patricia's killer, but I really don't believe that he could have done it. He was definitely a depraved individual, who might have gone on to commit even more horrific crimes if he had not been sent to prison (for a laughably short number of years), but I don't believe we can connect him to the Grimes sisters.

### The Killer of the Schuessler-Peterson Boys

At the time of the Grimes sisters' murders, most people in the Chicagoland region believed that the killer was the same person who had murdered the Schuessler-Peterson boys. And why not? The crimes were remarkably similar. The boys had been murdered, stripped naked, and their bodies had been dumped on the side of a remote, wooded roadway. The crime had shocked all of Chicago, perhaps even the nation. When two young girls were killed under almost the same circumstances, just a little over a year later, it seemed that perhaps a serial killer was at work.

When the police investigation into the murders of Barbara and Patricia began, nearly everyone involved, including Sheriff Lohman, believed they were looking for the same man. In time, opinions changed. The cases began to skew further and further apart until it became apparent to detectives that they were looking for another man entirely.

Over the years, though, there have been many who have suggested that perhaps the police were right in their first ideas about the two crimes. In addition to Kenneth Hansen, the man who eventually went to prison for the boys' murders, there were other suspects who it was believed may have also been linked to the Grimes sisters.

One of them was a man named Charles L. Dahlquist, a thirty-three-year-old golf caddy and former railroad switchman. In June 1957, he was arrested in Hollywood, California, after making an illegal U-turn in front of a police officer. When his plates were checked, it was discovered that his vehicle was stolen. Dahlquist was taken to Los Angeles Police Department headquarters, where he was questioned about the recent strangulation murder of a local nurse, Marjorie Hipperson, who was originally from Chicago. As details of the Dahlquist questioning filtered back to the homicide bureau in Chicago, Lieutenant Joseph Morris was assigned to coordinate local efforts with those of the LAPD.

As Morris began checking into Dahlquist, he discovered that he was a sexual predator who had jumped a $4,000 bond after failing to appear in Cook County Felony Court. The charge had involved indecent liberties with a fifteen-year-old boy at an Edgebrook golf course on August 22, 1955. He also discovered that after the Schuessler-Peterson murders, he had been picked up in Chicago because of an anonymous phone tip and was grilled by homicide detectives just hours after the boys' bodies had been found.

Additional information had been received about Dahlquist from Frank and Magdalena Kruell, a Northwest Side couple in their late sixties. They supplied police with new information that raised some startling questions. On July 15, 1955, the Kruells said that they observed a boy they believed looked a lot like Anton Schuessler, Jr. loitering with Dahlquist under the bridge that spanned the Des Plains River at Belmont Avenue. The couple explained that they were walking toward the bus stop when they noticed the man with the boy. It seemed very odd, and they reported the matter to the police after reading about the murders in the newspaper.

That stretch of Belmont Avenue, which is about two miles south of Robinson Woods, is a few hundred feet east of the Des Plaines River Road and about three miles southwest of the Idle Hour Stables. Even without these eerie links to the sites mentioned, it was a sparsely traveled country road in 1955 and not a place where a chance meeting would occur between a thirty-three-year-old man with a questionable history and an eleven-year-old boy would occur.

The unemployed caddy was seized on a warrant and taken to the Cook County State's Attorney's sex bureau for an interrogation. In a candid and revealing interview that failed to register with detectives, Dahlquist told them that he had previously worked at a greenhouse and nursery. Early in the case Detective Jim McGuire had been assigned to canvass Chicago-area floral shops and greenhouses, looking for a particular type of pronged garden tool that it was believed the killer had stabbed Bobby Peterson with.

On the night of the murders, though, Dahlquist said that he was home alone watching television from 8:00 p.m. until noon the next day. He vividly recalled the programs that he had watched that evening and even provided what turned out to be an accurate description of their content. The police were convinced that he was being upfront with them.

Dahlquist was put into a line-up for the Kruells at the detective bureau. The man and women were positive that this was the suspicious man that they had seen with the boy that summer. They were also sure that the boy had been Anton, Jr. "That boy passed within five feet of us on his bicycle!" Frank Kruell exclaimed. They said that both the man and boy ran off when they saw the Kruells watching them. Dahlquist flatly denied their claims.

Detectives questioned Mrs. Schuessler and asked if she remembered what her son might have been doing on July 15. Eleanor recalled that Anton had ridden his bicycle all the way out to Harlem and North Avenues on the West Side of the city. It was an astonishing distance for an eleven-year-old boy to travel alone. It is possible that Anton ended up near Robinson Woods, where he encountered Dahlquist by accident, or design. There have been claims made by some that Dahlquist had once worked at the Idle Hours Stables, but no real evidence of this exists. A Chicago newspaper noted that he had worked at a stable, but did not specifically mention the Idle Hours. But if he was at the bridge on July 15, who was the boy with him? Was it Anton Schuessler and, if so, what was he doing with a grown man of suspicious repute, so far from home? Was Anton engaging in improper behavior with this older man, or had he been lured into a sexual liaison that led to his murder?

Whether or not Charles Dahlquist was telling the truth about his whereabouts that day, he had no one to corroborate his story. Sporting a fashionable "duck's ass" haircut (Elvis Presley-style), Dahlquist was given three polygraph tests by the Chicago police. The first test cleared him, but the second and third tests were "inconclusive." Arraigned on an unrelated sex charge, he jumped bail and headed west. He was largely forgotten by the authorities in Chicago until he was picked up on the traffic charge. Dahlquist was no more forthcoming with the LAPD than he had been in Chicago in 1955. He indignantly informed the Los Angeles detectives that he had fled Chicago because he was tired of answering pointless questions about the murders. He said, "I'm not going to tell you anything more than I told the Chicago police!"

But, for whatever reason, Dahlquist decided to waive extradition and was sent back to Chicago. By the time of his arrest in California, more questions had come up about Dahlquist. In 1956, the three boys had been exhumed for further tests and the Chicago Crime Lab found particles of insecticides and grass fertilizer on their skin. Suspicion grew that the boys were killed inside of a greenhouse and there were still the scalp wounds on Bobby Peterson that suggested he had been "struck by a pronged garden tool."

Once he was returned to Chicago, Dahlquist was dragged before Chief Justice Wilbert F. Crowley to answer for the 1955 molestation charge. He pleaded guilty to a "crime against nature" and was sentenced to one to five years. No further investigation into his possible involvement in the Schuessler-Peterson case was carried out.

In hindsight, it seems very possible that Dahlquist might have been involved in the murders in some way. Linking Dahlquist to the victims, the area where he may have met with one of them, the proximity of the dump site, and the possible murder site, makes it possible that Dahlquist was a conduit to a sexual predator who took the boys to the Idle Hour Stables or that he met up with them earlier in the summer and introduced them to their pedophilic killer.

But what about Dahlquist's links to the Grimes sisters? According to author Richard Lindberg (who has written more about the Schuessler-Peterson case and about Chicago crime in general than any other living author), he spoke with Tony Wilson, a retired Cook County Sheriff's Police Department detective, who said that the name Dahlquist "sounded familiar," but he wasn't sure that was the suspect's name. Wilson explained that he and two other colleagues had opened cold-case files on the Schuessler-Peterson murders, the Grimes sisters murders, and the Judith Mae Andersen murder (which occurred in 1957 and is mentioned in the final chapter of this book). Wilson told him, "We had a lot of circumstantial evidence on one suspect in particular." They followed a man who worked in Brighton Park, Illinois, at a factory where employees worked with gasket-boring tools. The officers were certain that the hole in one of the thighs of one of the Grimes girls had been made with that kind of tool. Flesh had also been cut off the thigh of one of the Schuessler-Peterson boys, as well.

Wilson said that the man hung around the Habetler bowling alley on the Northwest Side and was a known homosexual and pedophile. His mother had an old cottage in the Fox Lake area and detectives learned that he lived there. They did a search of the cottage and found articles on the Schuessler-Peterson murders, the Grimes sisters, and Judith Mae Andersen. He added, "It was our opinion that this guy had a lot to do with their deaths."

But whatever secrets Dahlquist may have had, he took them to the grave. He died, long forgotten, in San Mateo, California, in 1991.

Tony Wilson's story didn't seem to involve Charles Dahlquist, but it was obvious that the police believed that the two cases were linked, even years later. A lingering question, though, is why would a pedophile suddenly change profiles and go from killing young boys to young girls? The murdered boys had been sexually molested and, as later revelations would reveal, the Grimes sisters were also raped. I suppose it's possible that a child killer would prey on either sex when it came to his victims, but what about Kenneth Hansen? Hansen, who was convicted of the murders, had a long history of molesting and attacking boys. Why would he have suddenly started raping and killing young women?

But here's a more frightening question: what if Kenneth Hansen didn't kill the Schuessler-Peterson boys? There was no physical evidence linking him to the crime after four decades. There were no eyewitnesses who saw him do it? What if this man, who was an admitted sexual predator, was convicted of the one crime that he didn't commit? He maintained his innocence to the end, although as any prison official can jokingly tell you, every prison is filled with "innocent me." It's worth pondering, especially when considering the letter that seemed to corroborate the suspect that was pursued by Detective Tony Wilson and his squad.

In time, with an absence of new leads and no promising suspects, the Schuessler-Peterson case went cold. A little more than a year later, though, the city was plunged into terror again when the Grimes sisters were found on the side of German Church Road. The police immediately began looking for a suspect and the car that he had driven on the night he abducted and killed the two girls.

In February 1995, Ray Gibson of the *Chicago Tribune* received a letter from a man that he had once attended grade school with in LaGrange. The man asked to remain anonymous, but the letter had to do with the Grimes murders. The man told Gibson that his father worked at the Fisher Body plant on Willow Springs Road. He had been coming home around midnight on the night that the girls had disappeared, and he saw this man that he worked with in his car. He was parked, with two young girls in his car, on 79th Street near Willow Springs Road. He witnessed a struggle in the car, but went on, thinking little about it.

The man he worked with lived in Balboa Trailer park and he had an auto body shop across from the Edgewood Country Club, next to a swimming pool and the other trailer park on Willow Springs Road. The man's name was Joe and he had not been to work that night.

The next day when he came into work, his face and arms had deep scratch marks on them. When he was asked about them, he said that a cat had scratched him. The car that Joe drove was unusual. It was made in the 1940s and had a split windshield. The anonymous man wrote, "The police did say they were looking for that type of car. After the police announced that, no one ever saw Joe drive this car again. Joe has since died."

The information in the letter fits a lot of what Tony Wilson told Richard Lindberg. Could the police have been tracking the same man that worked at the plant with the letter writer's father? Could the cases have actually been connected?

It certainly seemed that the shocking crime was a repeat of the events from October 1955. Ernest Tucker of the *American* wrote, "It was all the same. Chicago has lived through this before, just fifteen months ago, and the horror of that first shock has not yet worn off. The similarities are awful and obvious. So there was the question. Had the same killer who drove in Robinson Woods in October 1955 driven into the lonely road near Devil's Creek? If this is true, what lives among us? Who did these things?"

### The Killer of Roberta Rinearson

While similarities do exist between the murders of the Grimes sisters and the killing of Bonnie Scott and the Schuessler-Peterson boys, there is probably no other murder that so closely parallels the Grimes case than that of the Roberta Rinearson slaying eight years earlier. Roberta was a ten-year-old Brookfield girl whose body was discovered in a ditch on County Line Road, dividing Cook and DuPage Counties, on December 18, 1948.

There are uncanny similarities between the two cases. Roberta and the Grimes sisters were all products of broken homes. A movie theater figured prominently in both cases. On the day that she disappeared, Roberta left home at 5:30 p.m. to see a movie at the Park Theater in LaGrange, which was just a short distance from her Brookfield home. She was never seen alive again.

Her body was discovered the next morning in a ditch along the lonely roadway. A railroad bridge attendant named Clyde Sperry was walking to work and spotted a girl's green coat in a ditch. When he came closer, he

*Roberta Rinearson*

*Police officers at the scene where Roberta's body was discovered. Her body had been dumped along a remote road, far outside of the nearest town.*

saw arms and legs protruding out of the grass. He ran two miles to a gas station to notify the police.

Roberta had been beaten, raped, gagged with her own underwear, and strangled. She was dressed, however, still wearing her blue jumper from St. Barbara's Catholic School in Brookfield. Her clothing had been torn. Her bobby sox were pulled halfway off her feet. Her shoes were missing. A blue and white head scarf, apparently torn from her head, was beneath her body.

As the police arrived on the scene, they found automobile tracks in the soft earth of the shoulder, where the body was found. This led them to believe that the body had been dumped by an automobile. And it was the perfect place to do it. As investigators would find on German Church Road eight years later, the isolated spot offered no witnesses -- other than the dead of nearby Arlington Cemetery. A stretch of woods screened the road from the railroad tracks, and the closest house was about a mile away.

Roberta had gone missing the previous night. As mentioned, she was on her way to the movies, but never came home. Around 2:30 a.m., her older sister, Patricia, reported to the police that Roberta was gone. Roberta and two older sisters had been living for several years with their grandmother, Mrs. Anna O'Donoghue. They had no idea of the whereabouts of their parents, Robert and Eleanor Rinearson.

The community was, of course, shocked by the brutal crime and detectives immediately went into action. On December 20, a bartender named William Millay, who worked at the El Rando roadhouse, just north of Mt. Prospect, told police that he saw Roberta with a man on Friday night, just hours before her body was found. Millay was able to identify her picture for Sergeant John Selle of the Cook County Sheriff's Police.

According to Millay, the man who was with Roberta was thirty to thirty-five years of age, neat, and blond. He ate two hamburgers and then tried to buy liquor for the girl. Roberta was tall for her age, but she certainly didn't look old enough to drink. Millay refused.

Two hunters came forward to describe a battered automobile that they saw turn in front of them on County Line Road at about 3:00 a.m. on Saturday morning. They said that two men were in the car and that the hunters chased the vehicle for a short distance because the way that the men acted, "aroused their suspicions." The hunters did not know about the murder at that time.

Another report to the police said that a car fitting the general description of the one seen by the hunters was spotted near a creek about 7:00 a.m. on Saturday morning. Two young men, around eighteen years old, were also seen leaving the creek and rubbing their hands, as though they had just washed them.

On December 21, the case took a strange turn when a Mexican laborer named Herlindo Perez Arias, confessed to Roberta's murder in what officials called "vague terms." Arias had been picked by Hammond, Indiana, police while aimlessly roaming along a local highway. He attempted to escape when police turned him over to immigration authorities for questioning. While being asked about his citizenship status, he blurted out, "I choked that girl! I choked that girl but I don't remember much about it. I am foggy about it."

Arias was brought back to Chicago for questioning after he waived extradition, but authorities said very little at first about how much credence they gave his account. They later admitted that he told a "very incoherent story" and "refused to answer some questions as to details and said he didn't know other details."

Arias claimed that he stole an automobile in La Grange on Friday evening and a short time later, forced the girl to get into the car with him, drove somewhere, and attacked her. Later, he placed the body in a ditch and after driving for a while, abandoned the car.

Officials remarked, "He said he couldn't remember just what the automobile looked like or where he abandoned it."

The "confession" was quickly discounted, but would not be the last one that the police received. The next one would be much more troubling and likely resulted in the case never being solved.

Nineteen months after Roberta's body was found, the Lyons Police Department charged George "Whitey" Lettich, a thirty-six-year-old father of three, alcoholic, and thief, with the murder. The police held Lettich in seclusion for sixty hours while they tortured a confession out of him. The story, leaving out the beatings and torture, appeared in the newspapers the following day with a quote from Lettich: "I did it all right."

He had signed a 1,500-word confession that admitted that he had enticed the girl into his car, then raped, beat, and strangled her when she resisted his advances. He was charged with murder and arraigned before Police Magistrate Frank Kanelos in Brookfield. He was held without bail until his preliminary hearing.

Even on the day after the confession, some principals in the case were suspicious of his story. Grace Rinearson, Roberta's older sister, now twenty-one, told reporters: "If he did it, I hope they send him to the electric chair. But I know he's lying if he says that Roberta got into his car willingly."

Kidnapping, possible drinking in bars with older men, suspicious and conflicting sightings, rape, a body dumped on a secluded road, a questionable confession -- it all seems like a blueprint for the Grimes case, eight years later.

Lettich was prosecuted for the murder in 1951, but was spared the death sentence. His conviction was reversed on appeal to the Illinois Supreme Court. His sentence was eventually reduced to one to ten years in Stateville Prison in Joliet for sexual assault. However, one judge later said: "There is not a scintilla of evidence to connect Lettich with the crime except for his repudiated confession taken by police officials after he was kept incommunicado for sixty hours. I've read the opinion handed down by the Supreme Court in this case and I believe they should have not only reversed the verdict but should not have remanded it for retrial."

Whether or not George Lettich was the actual killer or the victim of the kind of brutal police tactics that were common in that era remains a mystery. We will never know for sure, but it seems unlikely. If he really was the wrong man, though, this means that the real killer walked free -- and may have killed again. Thanks to the rather remarkable similarities between Roberta's murder and the murders of Barbara and Patricia Grimes, it's not impossible to believe that they may have been killed by the same man.

### Murders of the Two Lost Girls

I have a lot of mixed feelings about a solution to the Grimes sisters' mystery. Honestly, I don't believe that we will ever know for sure who killed those young girls, no matter how much we try, how many theories are introduced, or how many new suspects are added to the mix. Sadly, I feel that too much time has passed for us to ever be sure about what really happened, but I do have some thoughts about the case.

Many still believe (myself included) that Bennie Bedwell was somehow involved in the crime. I think that Bedwell was too stupid to have been able to commit the murders and get away with it, so he would not have been acting alone. But I do think he was involved.

A lot of people disagree with me, and I understand their point of view, too. They think he was a drifter who was picked up by the police so that the case could have a quick resolution and go away. How could he have been at work that night (or was he?) and still grabbed the girls when they left the theater? He wasn't in two places at once, and yet, many believed he was still involved. We can dismiss Sheriff Lohman's theories since he had little investigative experience and was way over his head with the case, but what about the belief of Harry Glos? He was a former state trooper and had many years of police experience. He was sure that Bedwell was mixed up in the case.

And he was not the only one who thought so. There were other investigators who alluded to a connection between Bedwell and the Grimes sisters. In addition to the large number of witnesses who were positive that they saw them together, many McKinley Park residents spoke of being told to keep quiet about the questionable behavior of the two sisters. One man claimed that the girls actually hung around a bar near 36th and Archer. "Older guys would go inside and buy them drinks and deliver them outside," he said. "One of those guys was Bennie Bedwell." So, if Bedwell knew the girls, wouldn't it have been simple for one of his buddies to have picked them up after the movie at the Brighton Theater (while Bedwell was at work) and then meet up with him on West Madison Street, where they were seen together?

My personal theory is that this is likely what happened. No matter what you might think of the activities of the two girls and the behaviors that they allegedly engaged in, they did not deserve their horrible deaths. I have always found this to be one of the most heartbreaking crimes that I have personally researched. However, while I can only theorize about what the girls might have been doing and why they left home without telling their mother, I believe this is what happened that night.

I believe that the sisters were already acquainted with Bennie Bedwell and likely far too many of his shady friends. I believe that they had arranged to meet up with him after the movie that night and that they were picked up by one of his pals and taken downtown to Skid Row. The girls were playing at being grown-ups, drinking and dancing, and possibly even having sex -- as they had probably done on other occasions in the past. Why they stayed away from home for as long as they did (since Harry Glos proved that they could not have been killed before January 7) is still in question. However, there are clues that will be discussed shortly. I also believe that for at least part of that time, they were held against their will. I think that, at least for the next few days and nights, they were willing participants in their own disappearance. It probably started off as rebellion and attention-seeking and the sisters got in way over their heads.

At this point, I believe that Bennie Bedwell may have purposely hooked the girls up with a procurer for a prostitution ring. Whether this had been his intent all along is unknown, but there's no question that he was not exactly one of the smartest two-bit criminals in Chicago. He could have been coerced or convinced into working with someone who was interested in turning young women into prostitutes. Barbara and Patricia would have been seen as perfect candidates - young, seemingly innocent Catholic schoolgirls gone bad. The Southwest suburbs of Chicago were perfect recruitment areas and the location of a number of roadhouses and brothels during the 1950s. In fact, there was a known brothel located just over a mile from where the girls' bodies were found. From German Church Road to its location on Archer Avenue was literally less than a five minute drive.

Another location in Willow Springs was "Liberty Grove," a secluded area east of Wolf Road and north of Columbia Woods, where the nightly parties with prostitutes and their customers inside portable trailers was overlooked by the local authorities. Armed guards with shotguns were known to patrol the road leading into Liberty Grove. This disreputable trailer park was only a mile-and-a-half from the German Church Road crime scene and many believe it also might be linked to the murders.

It's possible that the girls were supposed to be taken there, or to another location in what was then remote Willow Springs, to be "broken in" as prostitutes. But no matter what kind of "fun" the girls had thought they were having, this is not something that I can see either one of them going along with.

Based on other accounts of young women who were essentially enslaved into prostitution, it was brutal. As the autopsy reports that were revealed by Harry Glos stated, the sisters had been held captive for several weeks and were repeatedly beaten, tortured, and sexually molested. It was probably soon very clear to the people in charge that the sisters were not going to willingly go to work for them. With more trouble on their hands than they wanted to deal with, the procurer, and possibly one or more of his associates, simply murdered the girls to keep them from talking about what they knew of the operation. Likely already stripped of their clothing in captivity, their nude bodies were dumped on the side of the road. If they weren't already dead by that time, they soon perished from exposure.

Some have suggested that the prostitution was heavily connected to organized crime and city politics, which might explain why the murders were never solved. Chicago doesn't exactly have a good reputation when it comes to police and political corruption. There could have been a number of people involved in the investigation who were paid to look the other way and to not look too closely in some areas or at certain people.

Where did this theory come from? Well, it became plain that there were just as many opinions about the characters of the two girls as there were theories about how they died. Descriptions of "pretty wild" were common with some of the investigators and with neighbors who knew them. By one account, the two girls "wore provocative clothes in the summer and flagged down cars full of boys." Many neighbors talked about the neglect they suffered and the lack of attention and discipline that they received from a mother who worked full-time and had problems with alcohol.

Many who knew them dispute the description of them being "shy," as their mother and the newspapers claimed. Most agreed that neither of the girls were shy. Another friend pointed out the amount of freedom that the sisters enjoyed when compared to the other young people in the neighborhood. One night, Barbara and Patricia came to a friend's house and invited her to go for a ride in their cousin's new car. It was 10:30 p.m. so her mother, unsurprisingly, didn't let her go. The next day, Barbara admitted to her friend that the guy with the car wasn't their cousin after all.

Some of the sisters' old friends believe that Barbara and Patricia, often left to their own devices by a combination of their mother's long work hours and drinking, were likely to have gotten into a car that night after leaving the theater. However, many of them feel that it might have been someone from the neighborhood - someone they recognized - who killed them. I don't necessarily agree that they were from the neighborhood. I think that, unfortunately, Barbara and Patricia had "friends" that their pals in McKinley Park knew nothing about.

Others have always refused to consider anything negative about Barbara and Patricia and were angered by the negative gossip about the two girls. A friend of Theresa Grimes said that the family was held together by love and hard work. She said, "Barbara and Patricia were nice, ordinary little girls, poor and happy; we all were. Their mother had to work, and she assigned them chores - mopping the floors was one. Our idea of fun was to pour soapy water over them and slide around in our bare feet, giggling, little kid stuff, you know?"

Many people in McKinley Park were angry about the negative gossip and some remain angry about this even today, maintaining that Barbara and Patricia were cheerful, ordinary, friendly girls, and were tragically killed on a cold night because they made the mistake of accepting a ride from a stranger. They didn't hang around in bars, these old friends maintain, they were simply innocent teenage girls, just like everyone else at that time.

I think they were nice girls. I think they were pretty, intelligent, and wonderful daughters who loved their mother very much, but who decided to rebel and made some bad choices - choices that tragically got them killed.

Truthfully, though, I'd prefer to think that their old acquaintances are right. There are few stories as tragic as the demise of the Grimes sisters and perhaps it provides some cold comfort for us to believe that their deaths were simply a terrible mistake, or the actions of a deviant killer. It can provide us that comfort of knowing that the girls were simply in the wrong place at the wrong time and that such a thing could have happened to anyone.

But does believing this make us feel better - or worse?

# HAUNTED BY CRIMES PAST

Many years have passed since the bodies of the Grimes sisters were found in 1957. A lot has changed in Chicago, in McKinley Park, and along the stretch of German Church Road where the girls' bodies were discovered by Leonard Prescott on that cold January afternoon. Of course, there is no statute of limitations for murder, so the case officially remains open. However, I'm not sure there is anyone -- no matter what claims are made -- who truly believes that it will ever be solved.

Little progress was made on the case in the years that followed. Rewards were never collected and the case went from cold to downright frigid. Then, decades later, hope was raised for the Grimes case when a solution was finally discovered to the Schuessler-Peterson murders from 1955. Bobby Peterson and the Schuessler brothers could finally rest in peace - but the same could not be said for Barbara and Patricia Grimes. Despite the new public awareness and police interest in their deaths, the case became cold once again. Apparently, the investigator's initial theories about a connection between their murders and those of the Schuessler and Peterson boys were not correct after all.

Now, almost sixty years later, the mystery of who killed the Grimes sisters remains unsolved. Those who still have an interest in the case will sometimes travel down German Church Road and wind up at the low point along this "haunted highway," where the bodies of the two girls were discovered so many years ago. Some say that the impact of the tragedy can still be felt there today - as if the impression of what may have been a depraved killer's most desperate moments somehow lingers behind.

The bodies of the Grimes sisters were tossed without ceremony at the edge of a ravine, just over a guardrail and only a few feet from the shoulder of the road. A short distance away from this site, its entrance once blocked with a chain, was a narrow drive that once led to a house that was nestled in the trees. Mysteriously, some say, the house was abandoned by the family who lived there soon after the girls' bodies were discovered. Many of the belongings were left

*The site where the Grimes sisters' bodies were found as it looks today. German Church Road has changed drastically over the last six decades as new housing editions have appeared along the road. It's hard to believe that it's the same place where the bodies were once found.*

behind in the house and toys and furniture lay scattered about the yard for years. Even a 1955 Buick sat rusting in the driveway, but it was eventually taken away. At some point, vandals set fire to the house and the owner had to demolish what was left. And while the owner never lived there again, people would occasionally see a tall, gaunt man roaming about the property in the spring and fall, when the trees and brush were thin. It was assumed that he had once occupied the place, but those who saw him were afraid to ask.

Until just a few years ago, the foundation of the abandoned house was still visible. The once landscaped hedges and a few remaining artifacts served to bear witness that a family had once lived here. Below the concrete slab of the house, a basement remained intact with a water heater, window screens, and an old workbench littering the crumbling floor. Today, the site is long gone. It has been replaced - as have most of the woods along German Church Road - with new subdivisions and homes.

Why the family abandoned this house remained a mystery for many years, but in 2005, I was able to interview Charles Werner, who once lived in this house with his family. His father, the "tall, gaunt man" who was often reported on the property, had been the owner and had been present on the day when the bodies of the Grimes sisters were found.

"The ravine where the Grimes sisters' bodies were found was very near the western property line of our house," Charles recalled for me. "My father had purchased the plot from a neighbor in 1947, or thereabouts, when my parents were first married. It was extremely rural at the time and my parents built a fairly large ranch house there. My sister was born in 1949 and I in 1951, and we spent the first years of our lives growing up in this house."

Mr. Werner, Charles' father, owned a successful plastic molding business and, because he was self-employed, typically stayed home during family vacations to maintain his business. Charles continued with his account: "It happened, in January 1957, that my mother had taken the two of us children on our yearly trip to Miami Beach, Florida. My father stayed home. I have a vague recollection - and I just talked to my sister who confirmed it - that my mother was extremely agitated reading the Miami newspaper. The paper had reported the Grimes murders, and had detailed the location where the bodies were found. Not surprisingly, this revelation upset my mother to quite a degree. Back in the middle 1950s, the murder of two teenaged girls in Chicago would make the front page of papers halfway across the country. It's sad to think of how numb we have become regarding such matters."

Charles' mother telephoned home and was stunned to learn that not only had the bodies been discovered on the road where they lived, but only a few feet from the edge of their property. His father had arrived home from work on the night the girls had been found and was "greeted" by sheriff's police officers with guns drawn at the entrance to his driveway. He was questioned about what he may have heard or seen, but he was apparently never seriously considered as a suspect.

Charles continued: "I don't recall any major upheaval in our family as a result of the murders. I was young, of course, and naturally, my parents would shield me from the lurid details of such a matter. I do recall friends of my parents breathlessly commenting on the 'Grimes girls' when they would visit. My parents did save the newspaper front pages regarding the story and I still have those to this day. My father's most vivid recollections following the murders involved the sheer number of thrill-seekers who paraded past the site in their automobiles and how he had to chase away people who came to our front door asking questions. I admit that I have no memory of these people. As far as I knew, things quieted down and I reverted to the blissful ignorance of my five-year-old life.

"That is up until the spring of 1957, when we were all 'reminded' of the incident..."

Each day, Charles' sister, who had just turned eight, would take her bicycle down the five-hundred-foot driveway to pick up the mail. Along the driveway was a large clearing and on one afternoon Charles' sister was surprised to see an unfamiliar automobile parked at the edge of the drive. Three men, apparently from the car, were walking around in the woods just beyond the clearing. They soon noticed her watching them and called out. Quite frightened, she abandoned the idea of getting the mail and hurried back to the house. Charles vividly recalled her entering the house and screaming about the men.

"My mother was never timid," Charles said. "She shooed us into her car, and took off down the driveway toward the clearing. The men were leaving just as we arrived, shooting gravel from under their wheels. My mother told my sister to remember the first digits of the license plate and told me to remember the last digits. We did so, and although the chase rapidly became futile, mother passed along the car make and license to my father, who reported it to the police.

"The men were apprehended and my sister had to appear in court to relate her story. The men denied having been there at all and accused my sister of lying, but the judge apparently believed her. I seem to remember they got off with a small fine for trespassing. I still recall that this outraged my mother who was convinced these men had known something about the Grimes sisters. After all, they were within fifty feet of the crime scene, just shortly after the snow cover had completely melted. Were they perhaps looking for some evidence that was left behind?

"We remained living in the house for another two years, through December 1959. My mother wanted us to be in a better school system, so she prevailed upon my father to rent, and then purchase, a house in LaGrange, which had excellent schools. I won't deny that the isolation was probably a factor in her decision and certainly the proximity of the murder scene didn't help matters in that regard. I know that it was always my father's intention to move back into the house, perhaps renovate it, and add a second floor. He always loved the house and the property, so he was never willing to sell it.

"His intention to move back explains why there were toys in the basement and a workbench still there. We never really 'moved out' completely and he would store things there that we didn't need in our LaGrange home. During the 1960s, he would generally go out there, do maintenance, and mow the lawn on Sunday.

"A building that remains unoccupied for long periods always seems to attract vandals and this house was no exception," Charles added. "It's a shame to think that each time vandals would break windows or knock down a door my father would go out and carefully repair the damage, only to find another problem the next time he went out. Finally, someone actually burned down the house completely. Even then, Dad gathered all of the limestone from the walls and carefully stored it in the garage. Today, at age 92, he still speaks fondly of the property.

"My Dad gifted the property to my sister and me sometime in the 1980s. I bought my sister's share from her shortly thereafter. When I moved to Mississippi with my wife in 1992, I decided there was no chance I would ever build there, so I sold it to a developer. There is a subdivision there now. No doubt most of the owners of those houses have no idea at all that they live merely feet away from the scene of what is arguably the scene of one of the most famous unsolved crimes of twentieth century Chicago."

Not surprisingly, the abandoned Werner house gained a reputation for being haunted in the years that followed, likely because of its eerie stillness and its proximity to the place where Barbara and Patricia's bodies were found. Could this have caused it to become haunted? The idea is not as far-fetched as you might think.

In the years since the discovery of the bodies, the police have received reports from those who say they have heard a car pulling up to the location with its motor running. They have also heard an automobile door creak open, followed by the sound of something being dumped alongside the road. The door slams shut and the car drives away. Reports claim people have heard these things - and yet there is no car in sight.

Another woman claimed that in addition to the sounds, she saw what appeared to be the naked bodies of two young girls lying on the edge of the roadway. She called the police, but when they investigated, there was no sign of any bodies.

According to author Tamara Shaffer, there was a young woman who took a number of her friends on a tour of the old Werner house and the murder site one evening. They walked up the path that branched off from the driveway and circled the ruins of the house, and under the light of the moon overhead they saw a car approaching up the gravel drive from the road. It was a dark vehicle, with no lights on, and it sped past them, drove around the house, and then disappeared. The woman and her friends decided to leave and as they did, they encountered two Willow Springs police officers, who had been called by neighbors to chase off the "tour group." The chain that had been used to close off the driveway was still hanging in place and, when asked, the police officers said that they had seen no other car. The "phantom automobile," as some have referred to it, apparently passed through the chain across the driveway and then vanished before it reached the roadway, where the police officers had been parked.

What lingers here along this roadway, after all these years?

Many researchers believe in what is called a "residual haunting," which means that an event may cause an impression to be left behind on the atmosphere of a place. If such things truly exist, it seems possible that the traumatic events surrounding the last ride of the Grimes sisters may have left such an impression on this small stretch of German Church Road. It may have also been an impression caused by the anxiety and madness of the killer as he left the bodies of the young women behind.

But believe in hauntings or not, that choice is up to the reader. But should you ever travel along German Church Road, I defy you to stop along that spot on the roadway where the bodies of Barbara and Patricia were found and I dare you to say that you are not moved by the tragedy that came to an end here.

Without a doubt, I think you will agree, no matter how the area has changed over the years - this is still a dark and haunted place.

# AFTERWORD

The story of the Grimes sisters' murder has always been a case that has intrigued me. I didn't grow up in Chicago and was certainly not around in the 1950s when the story made headlines in the city and across the country. I grew up downstate, blissfully unaware that this tragedy had ever occurred until I ran across a short entry about it in a Jay Robert Nash book about unsolved murders called *Open Files* in 1983. Intrigued by a case that wasn't too far from home, I learned what I could about it, but old newspapers files were not easy to come by for a high-school student in the 1980s. Of course, times have changed, and even though the Grimes sisters still only rarely make appearances in books, it's a lot easier to track down copies of the newspapers that were printed at the time. I know more now about this heart-wrenching case than I have ever known before.

Oddly, while living in Chicago for a few years, I actually lived just off West Madison Street. Skid Row has been gone for a very long time now and it's mostly new buildings, or rehabbed older ones, and the shabby bars, flophouses, and peep shows are definitely a thing of the past. But here's the weird thing for me - my house was right around the corner from the site of the old D & L Restaurant. I could have tossed a rock through the back window from my front stoop if it had still been there. I spent a few years very close to one of the last places that the Grimes sisters were possibly seen alive - and I had no idea.

I also remember my first trip to German Church Road and the bridge where the bodies were found. Back then (early 1990s), the road was still a very isolated place. The subdivisions that make up most of the road today did not exist then. There were no streetlights. It was a wooded, shadowy place during the day and very dark and forbidding at night. It was a place that I always described as feeling "bad." It just had a weird feeling about it. Was it because I knew what had occurred there? Perhaps that was it, I don't know, but it certainly left an impression on me and even today, I still remember how the road used to be. It's still a spot worthy of a visit, though, if for no other reason than to pay respect to the two young girls whose lives were so viciously cut short.

**News Report published on January 22, 1957, shortly after the bodies of the Grimes sisters were found.**

Recent visits to the Southwest Side have taken me not only to German Church Road but to the Grimes house on South Damen Avenue. It sold and re-sold many times over the years and went through a variety of owners. When I last saw it, it was well cared for and flowers had been planted in the tiny yard. I'm sure that whoever lives there now has no idea that it was once the center of Chicago's largest police investigation or that a grieving family once called it home. It's hard now to imagine this neighborhood in 1957, when reporters and police officers were camped outside the Grimes house and people were living in fear, wondering which of their children would be lost to them next.

Loretta Grimes died in December 1989 at a nursing home in Cicero, Illinois. She died from congestive heart failure, but it might as well have been a broken heart. She never really recovered from the loss of her daughters. She remained at the house on South Damen Avenue until the 1980s, sharing it at times with her son, Joey, and his family. She was buried near her daughters at Holy Sepulchre Cemetery in Worth.

Joseph Grimes preceded his former wife to the grave. He died after suffering a heart attack in June 1965. He was also buried at Holy Sepulchre.

Sheriff Joseph Lohman, despite his failure to solve the Grimes case, was widely regarded for his knowledge and understanding of social issues. During the 1930s, he and his wife had lived among Chicago's poor African-Americans and Italians in an effort to gain firsthand knowledge about urban problems, police work, and politics. He served on the faculty of the University of Chicago, where he was a dedicated and inspiring teacher. In addition to holding numerous positions in Illinois law enforcement, he organized and directed the first major study of race relations in the federal government. He served under Presidents Truman and Eisenhower as chairman for the National Planning Commission and helped establish the Southern Police Institute in Louisville, Kentucky. In 1958, following his term as Cook County Sheriff, he was elected treasurer of the state of Illinois. Unfortunately, though, Lohman's political aspirations clouded his judgment and, despite a good relationship with the press, his image faltered in the wake of the Grimes case. As predicted during his controversial tenure as sheriff, Lohman ran for the Illinois governor's office as an independent in 1960. He lost the election and moved to California. At the time of his death in 1969, he was the Dean of the School of Criminology at Berkeley.

Walter McCarron was elected to the coroner's office in 1952 and during his tenure, became embroiled in a number of controversial and politically volatile cases, including the Schuessler-Peterson murders, the Grimes sisters, and the death of merchant Montgomery Ward Thorne and Charles Weber, a former alderman in the 45th Ward. Prior to entering politics, McCarron was in the trucking business with his father and was the executive director of the Illinois Motor Truck Operators Association. He lived in Oak Park until he retired to Ft. Lauderdale, Florida. He was visiting relatives in Chicago at the time of his death, at age eighty-five.

Harry Glos, the assistant coroner at the time of the Grimes case, had an extensive history in law enforcement. In 1941, as a state trooper, he worked with a motorcycle team protecting celebrities who received death threats during war bond drives. The team, known as the Four Horsemen, also performed stunts on their Harley-Davidson motorcycles. Before joining the coroner's office in 1953, Glos had also been a patrolman in Forest Park and a sergeant for the Oak Park police department. When McCarron fired him after releasing information in the Grimes case, Glos continued to work on the case without pay. He later started his own detective agency and served as the chief of police in Northlake. Although he stood over six feet tall, weighed over 200 pounds, and was by all accounts both aggressive and forceful as a policeman, he also had a gentle and artistic side. He had turned down an illustrator's job with the Walt Disney Company in the 1940s, and later worked as a commercial artist who donated his time to do cartoons for the children's wards of area hospitals.

Glos retired for health reasons in 1986, and after a series of strokes, died in May 1994. A few months later, in August 1994, it was Harry Glos who played a pivotal role in making sure that three murder victims received the justice they deserved.

Shortly after Glos' death, his daughter, Renee, was going through his personal files, a voluminous collection of crime records that had been stored in the basement of the family's Oak Park home for years. She discovered a bulging folder of photos from the Schuessler-Peterson case, which she turned over to the Cook County state's attorney's office.

The files could not have landed on the state's attorney's desk at a better time. Investigators had been looking for graphic photos from the Schuessler-Peterson case ever since they arrested Country Club Hills stable owner, Kenneth Hansen for the boys' murders. There were few known official photos from the case and the Glos files were considered crucial to the prosecution's theory that held that the murders occurred in a barn owned by horseman Silas Jayne, who had been Hansen's boss in 1955.

At least one of the bodies in the photos appeared to bear markings or impressions similar to figures commonly used to decorate leather goods or a horse saddle. This prompted investigators to conclude that the body in question may have rested against the leather items after the murders were committed, but before it was disposed of, along with the others, at Robinson Woods.

Renee Glos said that unsolved homicides ate at her father. "He often worked long hours looking for that one piece of the puzzle."

As it turned out, many of the puzzle pieces Harry Glos found -- in scores of cases of violent deaths -- were routinely passed on to police detectives who were actively working the cases. But when he turned over photos, files, and leads, he kept a copy for himself, carefully cataloging photos and reports, so that he could keep chewing over the cases on his own time. Tucked away in his individual case folders were Glos' handwritten observations, hunches, and detailed drawings of crime scenes, which highlighted his artistic skill.

Even after his death, Glos had a hand in seeing that Hansen was convicted for the murders of the three Schuessler-Peterson boys, but he couldn't do the same for every case that haunted him. It was the Grimes case, never solved, that cost Glos his coroner's job and that he never stopped thinking about, all the way to his grave.

Harry Glos died, still wondering what happened to those girls -- and still convinced that Bennie Bedwell had somehow been involved in the murders.

Edward Lee "Bennie" Bedwell returned to Chicago for a short time after he was acquitted on rape charges in Florida in 1957. Later that year, he moved to Rantoul, Illinois, and returned to his carnival roots, operating a snake pit ride in a local carnival. As noted in an earlier chapter, he ran into trouble in Springfield, Illinois, in 1959, accused of theft and running off with the wife of his employer at a local junkyard.

In February 1972, he married Virginia Mae Irving at the Miracle Temple Church of God in Christ in Decatur, Illinois. I have been unable to learn if this was the same Virginia who had been married to

Casper Sullivan, the junk dealer from Springfield, but the first names are the same.

Virginia went to work in the carnival with Bennie, billing herself as the "Alligator Lady." The couple later moved to St. Louis, where Virginia grew up, and Bedwell worked as a truck driver in the construction industry. His difficult life, as well as his marriage, was short. Afflicted with diabetes, Bedwell died from heart failure in November 1972. Thanks to his brief military service, he was buried at the Jefferson Barracks National Cemetery in St. Louis. He was only thirty-five-years old at the time of his death - but he got about sixteen more years than the girls that he may have led to their deaths.

Aside from Loretta Grimes, perhaps the most haunted by the Grimes case were Leonard and Marie Prescott, the unlucky people who discovered the bodies of Barbara and Patricia Grimes in January 1957. They continued to live a few miles down the road from the body dump site, in the same house they occupied when the crime occurred, until they both died just ninety days apart. Marie died at age eighty-one in March 2005, after a fall from which she never recovered. For many years, she had cared for Leonard, who was diabetic and almost blind. Leonard died after a bout with the flu on May 2005. He was eighty-nine years old.

The couple, married since 1942, were no strangers to hard work, struggle, tough times - and to heartbreak. In the days that followed their grim discovery in 1957, they lost two children of their own. Marie Prescott always believed that Bennie Bedwell killed Barbara and Patricia. She came to this belief while attending the inquests held after their deaths. She resented the fact that the police had so aggressively intruded in their lives after they had reported the bodies. More than anything, though, she was haunted by what they had found that day. She was never able to drive down German Church Road again without thinking of that January day. It stayed with her for the rest of her life.

The cases of the Schuessler-Peterson boys and the Grimes sisters were not the end to the destruction of the innocent era in Chicago history. Even less remembered than the Grimes sisters were the deaths of Judith Mae Andersen in August 1957 and Bonnie Leigh Scott in 1958. Bonnie's murder was featured in an earlier chapter, but the death of Judy Andersen should not be forgotten. Her murder occurred less than nine months after the deaths of Barbara and Patricia Grimes and to this day, it has never been solved.

Judy, as her friends knew her, was just two months away from her sixteenth birthday and was preparing for her junior year at Austin High School when she left her home on Chicago's Northwest Side on Friday night, August 16, 1957. She was on her way to watch television with her best friend, who lived less than a mile away on North Central Avenue.

At 11:00 p.m., Judy telephoned her mother, Ruth, and pleaded with her to stay later to watch television, but her

*Judith Mae Andersen*

mother said no. And even though her friend offered to walk with her part of the way home, Judy left alone.

By midnight, Judy's parents were aggravated that she had not returned home. Angry at first, her father, Ralph, went out to look for her. He walked the distance between his home and the friend's residence, covering every route that he could imagine. There was no sign of Judy. His irritation turned into worry. At dawn, he called the police. A missing-persons report was filed, but the police were more inclined to treat the matter as a runaway, especially after her parents admitted that Judy had been refused permission to stay out later.

But Judy's friend didn't believe it. She came over to the Andersen house to keep a vigil with the family on Saturday afternoon. Consoling Judy's brothers, Bobby and Ralph, she told them, "Judy would never run away just because she couldn't watch an old movie. Your sister would never do that." Tragically, her friend turned out to be right.

147

Six days later, On August 22, boaters in Montrose Harbor, on Lake Michigan, north of Belmont Avenue and Irving Park Road, pulled ashore an old fifty-five barrel oil drum that they found floating in the water. They were stunned to discover that it contained the dismembered torso of a young woman. Her head, one arm, and both hands were missing. Without the head or hands, there was no way to immediately identify the body

*Lieutenant John Ascher of the Chicago Police Laboratory examines the 55-gallon steel drum that contained Judith's body parts, found in Montrose Harbor.*

and members of the Andersen family refused to believe that the corpse was that of young Judy.

Then, on August 24, a five-gallon pail was found floating near the shore. It contained a severed head, two hands, and one arm. Through dental records and fingerprints, the body was identified as that of Judith Mae Andersen. Before being decapitated, she had been shot in the head.

The police canvassed the area and found two fishermen with a story. Several nights earlier, while fishing on the other side of the harbor, they noticed the lights of a car backing down to the water's edge. A well-built man, too far away to identify, got out, opened the trunk, and threw several items into the water. As he drove away, they noticed that one of his brake lights was out.

As with the case of the Grimes sisters' murders earlier in the year, the search for Judy's killer became a massive manhunt. During the first year alone, 115,000 people were interviewed by the police, more than two thousand suspects were questioned, and seventy-three lie detector tests were administered. Police individually checked out one-hundred-and-fifty-two reports of shots being fired on the night that Judy vanished.

While this was taking place, police were also investigating a series of robberies and unusual sexual attacks on women on the North and Northwest Sides of the city. The attacks were nearly identical. The assailant confronted the women while they were walking alone, often just after they had gotten off the bus. He threatened his victims with a knife and then bound them with lengths of rope, each having the same number of twists in the braiding. Once secured, he cut the women, often around the genital area. Curiously, while the attacks were clearly sexually motivated, none of the victims were raped and no fluids were ever found at the scene.

Detective Chief Patrick Deeley formed a special unit that was made up of two hundred of the city's best officers to investigate the attacks. He placed Sergeant Charles Fitzgerald, a man known for putting in fifteen-hour days and among his peers as a "relentless pursuer of evil-doers," in charge of the task force. Fitzgerald had earned twenty-four creditable mentions as an officer, been cited twice for bravery by the City Council, and was recognized by the FBI five times. He had once solved a murder by piecing together a ripped up love letter that had been found in a garbage can. He definitely seemed to be the right man for the job.

Fitzgerald put the task force to work trailing buses from a discreet distance. It was not long before they spotted a car following a bus on Western Avenue, near Peterson. Because one of the car's tail lights was burned out, the officers had an excuse to pull the driver over.

The man behind the wheel was Barry Zander Cook, a stocky, boyishly-handsome, twenty-one-year-old construction worker. He clearly matched the description of the suspect who had been attacking women in the area, but not wanting to arouse his suspicions, the officers wrote him a ticket for the burned-out taillight and sent him on his way. Knowing his name and address, however, he was immediately placed under surveillance. Fitzgerald was sure they had their man, especially after it was learned that Cook had a previous arrest record.

The next step was for the victims to try and identify the suspect, without him knowing that the police were on to him. Investigators did this by secretly taking the victims to construction sites where Cook was working and having the women pick him out from among the other laborers on the job.

All went according to plan until February 26, 1958, when Cook recognized one of the victims. He started running, with four detectives in pursuit. They shot at him and when Cook was slowed down by a flesh wound in the leg, he was tackled by a detective.

He was taken to Cook County Hospital for treatment and, while there, it was discovered that he possessed immature genitalia, like that of a six-year-old boy according to reports, and he was unable to engage in normal sexual behavior.

Fitzgerald tried to interview Cook, but the suspect feigned unconsciousness for weeks, refusing to open his eyes or to speak to anyone but his father. This made it necessary for the police to bring the victims to the hospital to see the prisoner. To avoid criticism, police filled Cook's ward with thirty-five male patients, all in their early twenties and with the same basic physical shape of Cook. Police then brought in the victims, asking them to identify their assailant from among the patients. As a result of the identifications and witness statements, a grand jury indicted Cook with seven counts of assault with intent to rob, rape, and murder.

Thanks to the vicious and strange nature of the attacks, Cook also became the prime suspect in the murders of Judith Mae Andersen and Margaret Gallagher, a fifty-year-old beauty shop operator who was killed on July 23, 1956. She had been sunbathing in Lincoln Park, not far from where Judy's remains had been found.

Although Cook refused to speak to anyone but his father, Fitzgerald managed to convince the elder Cook that his son could be cleared of any suspicion in the homicides if he passed a routine lie detector test. But rather than clear him, the polygraph exam indicated that Cook had guilty knowledge of the murders of Judy and Margaret Gallagher -- just as Fitzgerald had suspected. The detective confronted Cook with the test results and gently suggested that he tell him about the murders. Cook agreed -- but only if his father told him that it was all right. Mr. Cook was not going to be fooled this time; he told his son not to talk to anyone.

Stymied, Fitzgerald returned the prisoner to the county jail. He was not ready to give up, though. Working secretly, he recruited Detective Anthony Muranaka, a slightly-built, Japanese-American who looked nothing like a stereotypical police officer, to go into the jail on phony charges to try and get close to Cook.

After several days in solitary confinement, Muranaka was transferred to "Murderer's Row," where Cook was being held. He soon struck up an acquaintance with the young man, and as the friendship grew over the next two weeks, Cook told the detective how he had murdered Judy and Margaret.

On June 23, 1958, facing a dozen witnesses who had positively identified him as their attacker in other cases, Cook entered a plea of guilty to the seven charges. He was sentenced to one to fourteen years at Joliet Penitentiary.

Fitzgerald and the task force had gotten their man, but the veteran detective wasn't giving up on clearing the two murders. He needed more details on the killings and Detective Muranaka was called on once again. On July 8, 1958, his head shaven, he was taken in chains, under heavy guard, to Joliet, where he was locked up in the same cell as Cook. The young man was relieved to see a familiar face and he took Muranaka into his confidence once again. Little by little, Cook told him everything that he needed to know.

Once Muranaka had gotten everything that he could from Cook, he turned it over to Fitzgerald. The detective came to visit Cook at the prison and told him everything that he knew. Cook, panicked, asked to speak to the warden on October 12, 1958, and poured out a full confession to the murder of Margaret Gallagher. Five days later, Cook was indicted for the killing.

In the spring of 1959, Cook was returned to Chicago for the Gallagher murder. It was an incredible proceeding that made banner headlines in all of the Chicago newspapers.

But it was the verdict that really shocked everyone.

Even though there was a witness who had observed the slaying through a telescope, Cook had failed the lie detector test, Fitzgerald testified to being present when Cook confessed Margaret's murder to his father, Muranaka told how Cook had confessed to killing a woman while she was sunbathing, and Cook confessed to Warden

Joseph Ragen at Joliet Penitentiary -- the jury found him "not guilty" after his parents testified that he was home with them at the time of the murder.

Unbelievably, Cook was returned to Joliet to finish serving his original sentence for the attacks on the other women. Muranaka's cover had been blown, so he was unable to get any more information from Cook. The Gallagher case could not be tried again, but there was still the possibility of getting Cook for Judy's murder.

Fitzgerald was sure that he had done it and even believed that he had figured out how Cook had committed the crime. Barry Cook's parents had been out of town on the night Judy disappeared. She may have tried to resist him. He then shot her in the head, and she died in the car. He then took her body home, undressed her, and cut her into manageable pieces. Fitzgerald believed that it had taken Cook a long time to do this and that he got "some kind of sexual gratification" from the macabre task.

To put it simply, "He enjoyed it."

He then sealed the torso into the empty oil drum and put the head and other body parts into the five-gallon bucket. He had to get the evidence out of the house before his parents returned from their weekend trip. He then hosed down the basement, making sure that things were "spotlessly clean."

It came as no surprise to detectives that Cook's family was refusing to cooperate with any further investigation. Unwilling to let that stop them, Fitzgerald and several of his detectives slipped into their home near Hermitage and Devon Avenues while the family was away visiting their son in Joliet. From the basement rafters, they recovered flattened slugs from a .32 revolver, consistent with the bullets found in Judy's head.

The house was bugged and soon, Fitzgerald learned that Cook's father had found the missing gun under some leaves beneath the front porch. Cook took a post-hole digger, dug a deep hole, and dropped the gun in it. He subsequently told his son during a prison visit, "I buried it where they will never find it, near the barbeque pit."

The cement foundation for that same backyard barbeque had been poured shortly after Judy's murder had taken place. Judy's clothing had never been found and Fitzgerald always believed that her clothing and shoes were under the concrete -- with the gun. But he could never get a warrant to search for any of it. His forays into the Cook house had been unauthorized and, technically, illegal. He could never offer the visit, or his listening devices, as a reason to obtain a search warrant.

However, until the time that he retired from the police department in 1964, Fitzgerald regularly visited Cook in prison. He always turned their discussions to the subject of Judy Andersen. Before he died in 1990, Fitzgerald said that Cook admitted to the murder: "He told me he killed Judy, but would not go into detail or give a formal statement. He said he could tell me a lot of things, but his father wouldn't allow it."

Barry Cook was released from prison in June 1967, after serving nine years for the attacks on the various young women. After that, the family moved to Houston, Texas. Fitzgerald continued to keep tabs on Barry, even after he retired. In 1973, when a twenty-three-year-old woman was stabbed, sexually assaulted, and left for dead in Houston, he provided the local authorities with information that led to Cook's arrest. Cook was also questioned about several unsolved homicides in the area, but he was never brought to trial.

In the end, Judith Mae Andersen's murder was never solved. Even though investigators were convinced of the killer's identity, there was nothing they could do to bring him to justice.

The Schuessler-Peterson murders shocked the public, the murders of the Grimes sisters baffled and horrified the city, the slaying of Judy Anderson shook the city to its core, and the brutal killing of Bonnie Leigh Scott dealt a fatal blow to any belief that Chicago was still a safe place for children to live.

It was the end of innocence in Chicago. The city - and the rest of America - was changed forever.

# BIBLIOGRAPHY

Baumann, Ed and John O'Brien - *Getting Away with Murder;* 1991
Chicago Historical Society
Halper, Albert - *The Chicago Crime Book;* 1967
Johnson, Curt - *Wicked City;* 1994
Kaczmarek, Dale - *Windy City Ghosts;* 2000
Lait, Jack & Lee Mortimer - *Chicago Confidential;* 1950
Lindberg, Richard - *Return to the Scene of the Crime;* 1999
--------------------- - *Return Again to the Scene of the Crime;* 2001
-------------------- and Gloria Jean Sykes - *Shattered Sense of Innocence;* 2006
Nash, Jay Robert - *Among the Missing;* 1978
---------------------- - *Open Files;* 1983
Newton, Michael - *Encyclopedia of Unsolved Crimes;* 2009
O'Shea, Gene --- *Unbridled Rage;* 2005
Shaffer, Tamara - *Murder Gone Cold;* 2006
--------------------- - *Unpublished / The Crime that Time Forgot*
Taylor, Troy - *Bloody Chicago;* 2006
---------------- - *Haunted Illinois;* 2004
---------------- - *True Crime: Illinois;* 2009
---------------- - *Weird Chicago;* 2009

*Personal Interviews and Correspondence*

**Newspapers:**
*Alton Evening Telegraph (Illinois)*
*Carbondale Southern Illinoisan (Illinois)*
*Chicago American*
*Chicago Daily Herald*
*Chicago Daily News*
*Chicago Herald & Examiner*
*Chicago Sun*
*Chicago Sun-Times*
*Chicago Times*
*Chicago Tribune*
*Chicago Public Library*
*Decatur Daily Review (Illinois)*

*Decatur Herald (Illinois)*
*Dekalb Daily Chronicle (Illinois)*
*Edwardsville Intelligencer (Illinois)*
*El Paso Herald-Post (Texas)*
*Freeport Journal-Standard (Illinois)*
*Galesburg Register-Mail (Illinois)*
*Harrisburg Daily Register (Illinois)*
*Ironwood Daily Globe (Michigan)*
*Logansport Press (Indiana)*
*Mattoon Journal-Gazette (Illinois)*
*Mt. Vernon Register-News (Illinois)*
*Oshkosh Daily Northwestern (Wisconsin)*
*Port Angeles Evening News (Washington)*

**SPECIAL THANKS TO:**
April Slaughter: Cover Design & Artwork
Lois Taylor: Editing & Proofreading
Lisa Taylor Horton and Lux
Orrin Taylor
Haven and Helayna Taylor
Rene Kruse
Rachael Horath
Elyse & Thomas Reihner
Bethany Horath
Dale Kaczmarek
Jim Graczyk
Richard Lindberg
Jay Robert Nash
Tamara Shaffer
McKinley Park Residents who asked not to be named
Former police officers who asked not to be named

And to all of those who have tolerated my fascination with this case for so many years. It's a dark and disturbing subject and if you're not bothered by it, there's definitely something wrong with you. But, I had a hard time shaking it. The young women in this book stuck with me and haunted my dreams, so this was a volume that had to be set free. I hope you were as interested in the story as I have been.

For "Petey"

CPSIA information can be obtained
at www.ICGtesting.com
Printed in the USA
FSOW04n0057210716
22900FS